Cycling
in
Oxfordshire

Susan Dunne

Published by Sigma Leisure – an imprint of
Sigma Press, 1 South Oak Lane, Wilmslow, Cheshire SK9 6AR, England.

British Library Cataloguing in Publication Data
A CIP record for this book is available from the British Library.

ISBN: 1-85058-405-2

Typesetting and Design by: Sigma Press, Wilmslow, Cheshire.

Cover picture: The Thames at Abingdon (Laurence Main).

Printed by: Manchester Free Press

Preface

Oxford is the unofficial cycling capital of Britain. Despite this, cycle touring literature on Oxford and Oxfordshire has so far been remarkable by its absence. In 1922 the local brewery, Morrells produced a "Hunting and Cycling Road Map of Oxford and District" with the intention of promoting local watering holes; Oxford City Council has produced a number of helpful leaflets aimed at the urban cyclist but little has been written for the cycle tourist in Oxfordshire.

This is a great pity – Oxfordshire is a beautiful and varied county, drawing as it does on the natural beauty assets of the Cotswolds, the Chiltern and the Thames Valley, the Vale of the White Horse and the Cherwell Valley. I have written this guide with a view to sharing some of the pleasures of cycling in Oxfordshire. Intended for the occasional as well as for the more experienced rider, the book contains 20 circular routes of varying distances including a section on the 200 mile Oxfordshire Cycleway. Each route has key information available at a glance to help you decide on a suitable route (see How to Use This Guide) and where possible I have indicated how routes can be lengthened, shortened or merged. On each route I have tried to indicate places of special interest. This is inevitably a selective choice – Oxfordshire is exceptionally rich in history, tradition, famous residents and stunning scenery and offers something for most tastes. One area where I have been unashamedly selective is in the choice of roads on each route – as far as it has been practical I have chosen quiet back lanes and minor roads avoiding the urban and seeking out the rural.

The tours given in this book are intended as starting points for exploring Oxfordshire by bicycle and need not be followed religiously. Serendipity and Cycling seem to go hand on handlebar – discovering something unexpected beyond the next hill, down an alternative pathway or through the next village is intrinsic to the pleasure of cycling so you may want to use this book as a rough guide rather than as a series of rigidly prescribed itineraries. Whilst I have tried to provide a selection of rides from all areas of Oxfordshire I have not aimed to be totally comprehensive in my coverage of the region – there are many more rides waiting to be explored. That said, the rides in this book offer an introduction to the cream areas of a beautiful county.

Many people have helped in the preparation of this book but a special thanks is due to Tracey Boylan who took valuable time off writing a thesis to provide the information on Wychwood Forest (Route 11), to the Cyclists Touring Club who have invariably been friendly, helpful and efficient when providing information, to DC Alan Deadman and the team at Oxford Police Cycle Department for the information on safety and security and for help above and beyond the call of police duty, to Nigel Coates, Oxford Cycling Officer and Keith Wheal of Oxfordshire Department of Leisure and Arts. Any mistakes are, of course, my own. And lastly many thanks to the man at Spokes Cycle Shop on the Abingdon Road in Oxford who did an emergency repair on my bicycle whilst I was researching Route 1 and refused to accept any payment – proof if ever it was needed of the cycling spirit.

Happy Pedalling!

Susan Dunne

Contents

THE CHILTERNS AND THE THAMES VALLEY

THE COTSWOLDS

THE CHERWELL DISTRICT

THE VALE OF THE WHITE HORSE

THE OXFORDSHIRE CYCLEWAY

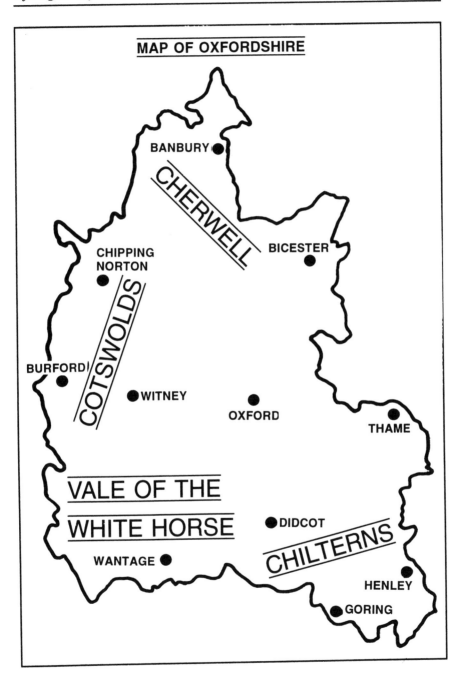

MAP OF OXFORDSHIRE

How To Use This Guide

Key Information

The rides are grouped roughly according to geographical location and are preceded by an overview of the history and geography of the area. Inevitably this has been a rather arbitrary process with some overlap and blurring of territories. These divisions are therefore for convenience of reference and are approximate. Each route in the book is circular and contains the following key "at a glance" information:

Distance: This is the basic distance for each route given. In practice, you will probably find some variation on this because of detours and short cuts. I have suggested specific means of lengthening and shortening the route after the mileage.

Maps: each route is accompanied by a basic sketch map, but I have included details of the relevant Ordnance Survey Landranger 1:50,000 (one and a quarter inches to one mile) map. Although most of the routes are self-explanatory and nearly all are adequately sign-posted a detailed map such as the O.S. is helpful in providing detail, assessing gradients and for any possible deviations you may want to take *en route*. A less tangible reason for taking a good map is the psychological boost gained from seeing how far you've come and where the nearest pub is likely to be.

Rail Access: With the exception of the Oxfordshire Cycleway, all the routes start and finish at or near a railway station. If you're fortunate enough to have a car with a cycle rack you can start the tours at any point (parking permitted). For those dependent on Public Transport see under "Getting there – trains, bicycles and Oxfordshire" on page 10 for details of train travel to and within the county.

Cycle Shops: Where possible, I have indicated the availability of cycle shops on each route in case the unfortunate does happen or you find you left home without a vital piece of equipment. Whilst every effort has been made to check that these cycle shops are operational, bear in mind that there is always the possibility of closure at a future date. Not all routes have a cycle shop and in any case you may find yourself miles from anywhere if you have a breakdown. See *maintenance and repairs* under "Hints for Touring".

Tourist Information: These are to help supplement the information given in this book. They can also offer help with local accommodation (see especially route 20).

Special Interest: Oxfordshire is well endowed with places of unique interest. Ranging from the whimsical Well at Stoke Row to the splendours of Blenheim Palace, from natural beauty spots to urban constructions, each tour offers one or more attractions on route.

Refreshments: I have indicated where possible the availability of refreshments and pubs serving food on each route. This is by no means exhaustive but, as with cycle shops, it should be born in mind that some places may be shut on the day you are cycling. If you are planning to stop for a pub lunch it is a good idea to check that food and drink will be available on the relevant day. Most watering holes can be found in the Yellow Pages or through Directory Enquiries.

General Description: In addition to the key information I have included a brief general description of each route indicating points of interest and types of terrain. This is to help you decide on the suitability of the tour to your needs.

Cycle Touring Tips

If you're an experienced cycle tourist you will probably want to skip this section and go straight to the routes themselves. Most of what follows is just common – cycling – sense but if you're new to touring or tend to use your bike as a means of urban transport a quick read through this chapter may help you avoid some of the pit falls that more seasoned cyclists have found out to their cost.

What to Take

The answer is as little as possible – less some. Cycling should be as light and easy as possible and excessive baggage is a hindrance. Weight slows you down, tires you more easily and hinders your enjoyment. The majority of rides in this book are intended to be completed in a day so kitchen sinks are not strictly necessary. A suggested basic list is:

1. Food and Drink (transfer glass bottled drink to plastic containers where possible).

2. Bicycle Repair Kit (see under *Maintenance and Repairs*) and Bicycle Pump

3. Waterproofs

4. An extra layer of clothes to put on/take off

5. Map

6. This book (or better still, photocopy the relevant section)

What to Take it in

The main consideration when carrying items on a bicycle is that the weight should not hinder your movement or upset your balance. Generally it is best to carry weight on the back of the bicycle in a basket or better still in pannier bags. To use panniers you will need to have a cycle rack fitted over your back wheel (you can also get extra panniers to go over your front wheel). Any initial expense is usually offset by having the ready equipment for any tours you may want to make in the future.

If you're travelling with one or more persons, the weight can be distributed around and some items like repair kits can serve several people. Another useful, but by no means essential piece of carrying equipment, is a small handlebar bag – handy for quick access to cameras, maps, chocolate, drink, cash...

Carrying your "stuff" in a shoulder bag or knapsack is feasible but less than ideal – shoulder bags can be unbalancing and carrying a bag on your back is more tiring. That said, don't be put off cycle touring by lack of the ideal equipment – you can always buy more at a later date.

When to Go

You can cycle all year round. In popular imagination cycling is often associated with golden summer days when the weather is (in theory) at its best and everything tends to be open. Cycling can be just as enjoyable in the more temperate weather of Spring and Autumn and even in the more bracing winter weather too. In cycling you become aware that each season has its own peculiar merit and charm – no season compares with Autumn for riding through woodland or with Spring for seeing the earth come back to life again whilst riding through a world transformed by snow and hoar frost in Winter can be one of the most enjoyable cycling experiences of all.

What to Wear

Your enjoyment of rides will, to some extent, be affected by what you wear. Oxfordshire is a fairly mild temperate region and extremes of temperature are rare but parts of it are hilly and exposed. As well as enjoying the elements through cycling you need to be adequately protected against them and being too hot or too cold can impair your cycling performance. The answer lies in layers of clothing – always take enough clothing to take some off or put some on according to need. In cold weather wearing a hat reduces heat loss from the head as well as protecting your ears and wearing two pairs of gloves and socks can help protect other extremities. Bear in mind also the wind-chill factor. You may work up a sweat going up hill but you can catch quite a chill from riding downhill into the wind. Wind can also slow your progress so if it's very blustery you may want to moderate the distance you travel. Given the perversities of the British Climate it's usually a good idea to take waterproofs whatever the season (except in a heatwave and even then . . .). Cycling whilst soaking wet can be less than pleasant. In Summer take care against overheating and exposing your skin to the sun too much too soon. Riding all day in sunlight can be a strain on the eyes – sun-specs can be useful.

If you give some thought to weather conditions before you start your journey you should be able to enjoy the ride whatever the season.

Food and Drink

Cyclists need fuel for energy – it's as simple as that. Whole academic treatises have been written on the principles of nutrition and cycling performance but the basic principle is that a good supply of food (especially carbohydrates) and drink is essential when out cycling for long periods. If you find yourself running out of energy on a ride it's probably because you need to take a break and eat and drink.

Make sure you have adequate food and drink supplies with you. Whilst all the routes in this book have food shops and/or pubs along the way there's always Sundays, Bank Holidays, owner moved or closing time to consider. Being caught out without food and drink is not funny – this is the fuel that will get you there and back. Short of abandoning your bike and hitching home you are totally dependent on your own steam. It is usually best to eat and drink regularly on the way and remember that it is not just in a heatwave that you lose body fluid you need drink regularly at any time of the year even if you're not particularly thirsty. The affect of the humble cheese sandwich on my cycling energy levels has never ceased to amaze me.

Pacing It

The amount of cycling you do in a day won't always depend on your level of cycling fitness. If you regularly cycle to and from work or use your bike frequently you'll be better equipped to take on longer distances but there are other factors to take into account. Extremes of temperature, hilly terrain, the speed you ride at and the amount of time you allow yourself to complete a journey all play a part in determining the length of ride you can comfortably undertake.

Cycle touring is a leisurely activity which should be done at a pace that is comfortable to you. If you're riding in pairs or in a group agree to meet up later along the way if necessary. Allow enough time and if you need a break use your brakes. Get off and stop, talk to the cows, feed a horse, admire a church. Regular stops also prevent you from becoming stiff from maintaining the same position for too long.

If you are in doubt as to your cycling endurance start with a short ride and take it from there.

A Word about Hills

Some cyclists feel duty and honour bound to ride up every hillside. This duty and sense of honour are entirely self-imposed. If it's more comfortable to walk up, then walk. There are a number of steep hills among the rides contained in this book and even those with double digit gears may find it a strain from time to time. The idea is to enjoy the rides not to emulate the 'Tourers de France'. And remember – for every up there's a down.

Which Cycle?

Most bicycles are suitable for touring – some people even do it on tricycles. For these rides ordinary tourers or racers are fine and you don't need a mountain bike costing thousands – and with almost as many gears – to complete these rides comfortably. That said, your ride will be easier if you have a good selection of gears. Whilst most rides in this book can be completed with five gears, ten would be more comfortable and more than ten an asset.

Maintenance and Repairs

Most of the routes in this book have a cycle shop on them at some point but this is of limited help if you find yourself stuck on a hillside with a breakdown. It is beyond the scope of this book to serve as a repair manual but certain very basic maintenance procedures can help both with ease of cycling and as a precaution against breakdowns. Before you go check for loose nuts and bolts, oil the chain and make sure the tyres are pumped up hard. The last two make for a smoother, easier ride. Keeping the bicycle clean and the moving parts well lubricated all year round helps too.

Many cycling books suggest that you take a puncture repair kit and a few tools. So does this one, but with the added suggestion that you learn how to use them first. If you don't know how to repair a puncture, find out how to now rather than when stuck on a remote hillside. Cycling is an independent activity and part of the independence lies in being self-sufficient when it comes to breakdowns. A well-maintained bike is less likely to break down, but it could happen – having some knowledge about the whys and wherefores of bicycle mechanics contributes considerably to peace of mind when touring. If you can't find anyone to teach you, buy a manual. Recommended is "Cycle Repair, Step by Step" by Rob van der Plas (Springfield Books Ltd) which has good illustrations and no nonsense explanations. You can also take a cycle repair/maintenance book with you such as "Roadside Bicycle Repairs" by the same author (Bicycle Books, San Francisco).

A Suggested Basic Repair Kit:

1. Puncture Repair Kit, tyre levers and pump (in practice it's often easier to take a spare inner tube to save time on repairs)

2. Multi-purpose box spanner or adjustable spanner

3. Spare brake and gear cable

4. Set of assorted Allen keys

5. Small screwdriver

Cycling Safety

BE SEEN, BE SAFE is a slogan that has stood the test of time – and with good reason. Cyclists need to be visible and this is particularly true on unlit country roads. If you are cycling out of daylight hours or in less than ideal visibility conditions a front and rear light are essential. The introduction of the flashing rear light has much to recommend it but this should legally only be used in conjunction with a full beam rear light.

The more reflectors and luminous strips you have about you the better. The pay-back for what may seem to be a Christmas Tree effect could be your life. Bear in mind that in winter you have fewer daylight hours at your disposal. Cycle helmets are not compulsory but are recommended for head protection. Cyclists are as bound by traffic regulations as car users.

Security

The days when you could just lean your bike against a wall and leave it are long gone. Whilst this is particularly true in the cities, villages and rural areas are not the safe havens they once were. If you're leaving your bike unattended lock it. No lock is infallible – even the mighty D Lock can be picked in minutes – but locks do serve as a deterrent. Always lock your bike to an immovable object which can't be picked up and carried away.

In cities and towns it's not a good idea to leave panniers and accessories on an unattended bicycle but, unless you're very unfortunate, it should be alright in the countryside and the villages for short periods of time.

For further details on how to make your bike more secure see under Cycle Security in Oxford (Next Chapter).

A Word about Horses

Oxfordshire is a rural county and sooner or later you're likely to bump into (metaphorically speaking) horses on route. The silent approach of a bicycle is potentially more disturbing to a horse than the well announced sound of a car. Bear this in mind when over taking horses – allow riders time to pull over and stop and give the horses adequate clearance space (preferably by cycling on the opposite side of the road).

OXFORDSHIRE:
a brief introduction

Set to the south of the Midlands and situated in the Thames Basin and its tributaries Oxfordshire is a relatively low lying county whose geography is particularly fortunate. From the flat lowlands of the Vale of the White Horse, overlooked by dramatic chalk down-lands and the Ridgeway, and the beautiful beech woods of the Chiltern Hills, from the rolling patchwork hills and golden stone villages of the Cotswolds to the deep valley of the River Cherwell and the low lying plains of East Oxfordshire, you are never allowed to feel that you are simply seeing more of the same. To cycle through Oxfordshire is to experience the subtle and dramatic changes of landscapes at first hand. Oxfordshire is hallmarked by peaceful villages and small market towns with Oxford itself providing the only major city in the county.

As with the landscape, traditional craft and industry within the county are astonishingly diverse. Whilst much of it has now disappeared Oxfordshire still retains links with its heritage as seen in the blanket making industry in Witney and brewing at Hook Norton. The Cotswold Wool industry on which the area grew rich has had its heyday and the area is now better known as a tourist attraction of England at its prettiest. Glove making at Charlbury and Woodstock, pottery at Leafield, lace-making at Bicester and around Banbury, stone quarrying at Headington and chair leg making in the Chilterns, to mention only a few of Oxfordshire's traditional crafts, are now largely things of the past but vestiges of this rich heritage can still be found in museums and place names on these routes.

More tangible links with the past can be seen in the presence of the Oxfordshire Canal running through the Cherwell Valley. Completed in 1790, the Oxfordshire Canal linked the City of Oxford with Banbury and the industrial Midlands. Its effect was the breaking down of dependence on local markets by opening up Oxfordshire to a wider area of trade. Further south in the Vale of the White Horse, the advent of Brunel's Great Western Railway (GWR) coming to Didcot in 1841 followed by a branch line to Oxford three years later further opened up the County to "outside" influence. In the early twentieth century the Morris Motor Works at Cowley (see under Oxford) transformed Oxford into a major motor manufacturing city. Set against all this change has been the unwavering position of Oxford University which has been the realm of hallowed academia since the 12th century.

Or take it by boat? The Thames near Day's Lock, Dorchester.

Getting There – Trains, Bicycles and Oxfordshire

Oxfordshire's central position means that it is fairly well-served by a network of trains. There are frequent intercity services to Oxford, Didcot and Banbury from London and Birmingham. The Cotswold stations in this book (Kingham and Charlbury) enjoy the regular service of the Cotswold regional railway which leaves from London Paddington and passes through Oxford, finishing at Hereford. The stations on the Chiltern routes at Goring and Cholsey are also frequently served by trains from Oxford to Reading. The south western section of Oxfordshire is less fortunate and route 19 (western section of the Vale of the White Horse) involves a trip over the county border to Swindon in Wiltshire. Services to Bicester (Route 17) are limited and rumoured to be under threat.

Regulations regarding cycle carriage on trains are complex and seem to be in a constant state of flux. On some trains you may be expected to pay a carriage fee of £3 per single journey and some trains will not carry bicycles at peak commuter times. In practice I have never been prevented from travelling anywhere in Oxfordshire with a bicycle and only rarely had to pay the carriage fee. Further details can be obtained from British Rail.

Oxford – a Cyclist's City

An estimated 20,000 cyclists skim through the City of Oxford daily. This gives it one of the densest cyclist populations in the country, with only York and Cambridge achieving similar numbers. 19% of the city's population cycle to work compared with a national average of 2%. Whilst a significant proportion of these may be students, many city dwellers daily take to two wheels as the quickest, most economical and most environmentally friendly form of transport.

During the heyday of British cycling in the late 19th and early 20th century cycling clubs in Oxfordshire were numerous but the bicycle has retained its popularity in Oxford despite its subsequent waning fortunes in other parts of the country. Both the University and the City have active cycling clubs and the Oxford Cycling Campaign (CYCLOX) seeks to promote cyclists rights within the City. The relative flatness of the City area (despite the steep incline of Headington Hill), the cycle's popularity with students as a cheap and quick means of dashing from bedroom to lecture theatre in the morning, and an image of accepted tradition have all contributed to the bicycle's continued popularity in Oxford. As much a part of the scenery as the famous Oxford skyline, the bicycle is popular with all sectors of the community from gowned dons to grandmothers.

Tom Tower, Christ Church College

It is perhaps ironic in these days of concern over the impact of the motor car on the environment that the founder of Oxford's motor industry, William Morris (later Lord Nuffield) should have begun his career as a manufacturer of bicycles. Born in 1877, Morris left school at 14 to become apprenticed to a bicycle repairer. Soon, with only £4 of capital, he set up his own cycle repair shop in a shed at his parent's house in Cowley. From repairing he moved on to building cycles and took up cycle racing, becoming the local cycle champion by 1901. He went on to set up shop at 48, High Street, Oxford and then moved on to motorcycles and into bigger premises at the corner of Hollywell and Longwall Street. From motorcycles he progressed to motor cars and the first "Morris Oxford" was born in 1913.

Urban Cycling

Morris had moved on to bigger if not necessarily better things but the bicycle was here to stay. Oxford City Council has long recognized the need for special provision for its large numbers of cyclists and employs two cycling officers to help promote its policy of encouraging cycling provision and cycle use in a framework of safety. The cycle parks at Westgate and Magdalen Street were set up as early as 1935 by the Council and more recent innovations include the Advance Stop Line for cyclists at the junction of Parks Road and Broad street. This was the first to be introduced in Britain and allows cyclist to wait at the traffic lights in a reservoir area in front of cars. The Council has also been active in promoting cycle commuter routes, one of which forms the basis of Route 3 in this book.

For further details of facilities for urban cycling in Oxford see the leaflet "Cycle Into Oxford" (cost 25p) available at the Tourist information Centre in St Aldates and at the Town Hall opposite and also stocked by some Cycle Shops. Produced by Oxfordshire County Council, the leaflet gives details of cycle routes, cycle lanes, cycle safety and cycle shops in and around Oxford.

Cycle Security in Oxford

What follows is not intended to put you off cycling in Oxford but to help prevent theft and bike loss by suggesting some basic security measures.

Over 3,000 bicycles a year are stolen in Oxford – enough to keep a Police Cycle Department staffed by four people busy throughout the year. Although the Department is able to recover approximately half that number, the fact remains that cycle theft in Oxford is epidemic (even the Lord Mayor of the City has had his bicycle stolen and whilst the Cycle Department managed to recover it within days it does prove that it can happen to anyone).

The Department recommends outside the Town Hall or outside the Police Station (both in St Aldates) as the safest places to leave a bicycle in Oxford. The Youth Hostel in Jack Straw's Lane is also good as it provides facilities for locking away cycles. Safety, they say, is not necessarily found in numbers and the large cycle parks outside the Railway Station, in Gloucester Green and Magdalen Street are common stalking grounds for thieves. Leaving a bicycle in town over night is also best avoided.

Lock it or Lose it

Wherever possible cycles should be locked up and locked away – the Cycle Department recommend a good D-Lock which should be attached to an immovable railing (or similar artifact) to prevent thieves from picking up the bike and carrying it off. In the annoying event of you losing the keys to your lock the Cycle Department will have it unpicked for you free of charge.

Another valuable service provided by the Cycle Department is the postcoding of bicycles which is available every Saturday morning. This can considerably increases the chance of getting a stolen bike back and the postcoding system can be checked anywhere in the country. Distinctive stickers or a personal imprint also help in the recovery process.

The Cycle Department operates a Green Card System whereby anyone wanting to sell a bike to an Oxford dealer must produce a Green Card as proof of ownership. This has helped cut down the traffic in stolen bikes in the City but bicycles are also sold out of the county and between individuals.

If the unfortunate does happen report it straight away – this increases the chance of recovery. Every year the Police auction van loads of recovered stolen bicycles which have simply not been claimed. In recent years the Cycle Department has returned bicycles to overseas visitors from as far afield as Switzerland, Australia and the United States.

Further details, advice and enquiries on cycling security can be obtained from the department, headed by cycling's Inspector Morse, Detective Constable Alan Deadman (see Appendix for address).

Bicycle Hire in Oxford

Many students in Oxford hire bicycles for the duration of a term and this is a popular means of getting two wheels. Demand for hire bicycles is high and this is true even during the Summer Vacation when the outflux of students is counterbalanced by an influx of visitors. Whilst high demand may limit the availability of bikes for hire, it does make the cost competitive.

The average cost is currently £5 per day. Not all shops will hire for a day with many preferring to hire for a week. The average weekly cost is £10 which makes it more cost effective. You will also be expected to pay a deposit (averaging £25). Details of Cycle Shops hiring bicycles can be found on the "Cycle into Oxford" leaflet (and see Appendix).

Cycle Repair

There are seemingly numerous cycle shops in and around Oxford and again details can be obtained from the "Cycle into Oxford" leaflet (and in the appendix). Particularly recommended for efficiency, expertise and a customer-friendly approach is: Bee-Line Bicycles, 61 – 63 Cowley Road, Oxford. Tel: (0865) 246615

The Visitor to Oxford

If you are passing through Oxford as part of a cycling trip or using it as a starting point for a cycle ride you will almost certainly want to spend some time enjoying its treasures. The visitor to Oxford faces a dilemma – where to begin sampling the pleasures of this beautiful, historic City. The answer lies to a large extent on individual interest. Whilst it is beyond the scope of this book to provide a comprehensive guide to Oxford, the following highlight some of the City's major attractions:

Colleges

There are 35 Oxford Colleges, many of which are in the City Centre and are open to visitors. Whilst they all have unique points of interest and many of them are architecturally stunning the show piece tends to be Christ Church in St Aldates with its own Cathedral. Cycling is generally not permitted in College grounds.

Museums

The Ashmolean Museum in Beaumont Street is the oldest Museum in Britain with collections from antiquity, galleries of sculpture and painting and displays from Egyptian times and the Middle Ages. The Pitts Rivers Museum and the University Museum, South Parks Road contain fascinating collections from natural history (including dinosaur skeletons) and anthropology. Visit the Museum of Oxford, St Aldates, to discover the history of Oxford (both the city and its university).

Gardens

The Botanic Gardens, Magdalen Bridge: set beside the banks of the River Cherwell (where you can also go punting in Summer), this is a former medicinal garden and is now used by the university for teaching and research into Botany.

Christ Church Meadows, St Aldates: beautiful gardens in the shade of Christ Church College and leading down to the banks of the Thames. Great for a picnic.

Academia

The Bodleian Library, Broad Street: the University library dates back to 1602 and is one of Britain's copyright libraries. Guided tours available.

The Sheldonian Theatre, Broad Street – the great assembly hall for University functions. Magnificent architecture.

Accommodation

This is fairly plentiful in Oxford, but not cheap. There is a Youth Hostel at Jack Straw's Lane, and a camp site (Camping International) behind Touchwoods Sports Shop near Abingdon Road. For further information contact the Oxford Tourist Information (see Appendix for address).

ROUTES 1 – 7

Starting from Oxford

Note: all the routes in this section start from Carfax Tower at the crossroads of Cornmarket Street, Queen Street, High Street and St Aldates. To get to Carfax from the railway station, turn left as you leave the station into Park End Street where you veer left at the junction into the one way road which veers round to the right into Hythe Bridge Street. Take the right-hand lane of this one way street and turn right into Worcester Street. Keep to the left-hand lane and turn left into New Road. This takes you up to the shopping precinct where you wheel your bike through Queen Street and Carfax tower is on your left.

Route 1:
Oxford – Kennington – Boars Hill – Cumnor – Oxford

Distance: 15 miles.

You can reduce the distance by about five miles if you turn right at the roundabout at the end of Abingdon Road (A34) and continue straight up, across the next busy roundabout towards Boars Hill. You can extend the route by crossing straight over the B4017 to Tubney and Fyfield and rejoining the route via Appleton at Cumnor.

Map: Ordnance Survey Landranger 164.

Rail Access: The journey starts and finishes in Oxford.

Tourist Information: Oxford, St Aldates.

Cycle Shops: See appendix under Oxford Cycle Shops. *En route* is "Spokes Cycles", 319 Abingdon Road.

Special Interest: Jarn Mound, Boars Hill.

Refreshments: The Flowing Well Pub, Sunningwell.

General Description

This route takes you to a view of one of England's best-known skylines – Matthew Arnold's Dreaming Spires (see under Boars Hill). Ascending out of Oxford to the wooded hills of Cumnor and Boars Hill, it takes you to Jarn Mound (see below) and to the hallowed residential area of Boars Hill – home to a quatrain of famous poets and host to many more. Despite its proximity to the city this is a peaceful area of hills and woodland. Most of the climbing is gentle although the stretch beyond Bayworth which takes you up Foxcombe Hill may reduce you to a short walk. The ride ends with an easy cruise down Cumnor Hill into the centre of Oxford.

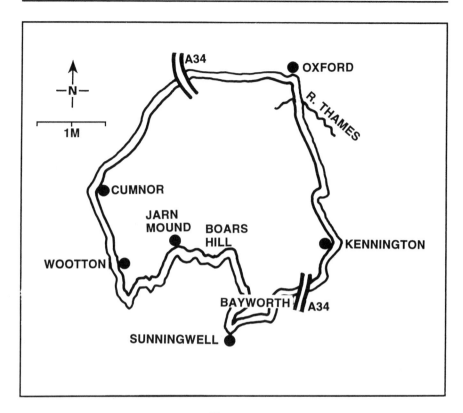

Route

Starting from Carfax Tower, turn into St Aldates which descends gently past the Town Hall and Christ Church College on your left and the Tourist Information Centre on your right. Carry on over Folly Bridge and the River Thames where the road merges into the Abingdon Road (A4144). Continue to the end of Abingdon Road (nearly two miles), joining the cycle path which runs along the pavement just after the Rivermead Rehabilitation Centre on your left. By staying on the cycle path you can avoid the busy roundabout at the end of Abingdon Road. Instead turn right under the roundabout subway and veer left under a second bridge which will bring you out onto the pavement parallel to the Ring Road. Carry straight on for about 500 yards until the signpost left to Kennington and views of hills and Bagley Woods.

The view from Folly Bridge, Oxford

Turn left and carry on to the end of this slip-road and turn left again into Kennington Road to go through the Oxford suburb of Kennington with its traffic calming humped zebras. After about a mile turn right, past the War Memorial into Bagley Wood Road. This narrow wooded lane rises then descends to bring you out at the junction of St Swithuns Road where you turn right, staying in Bagley Wood Road. Follow the gradual rise up the hill through Bagley Woods then cross over the Bridge with the busy A34 beneath you.

At the end of Bagley Wood Road, turn left at the give way sign and continue for about a third of a mile to the crossroads. Turn right, following the signs to Sunningwell and follow this road flanked by hills and trees. Oxford is only five miles away but there is a definite sense of being in the open country at this point. The impression is betrayed somewhat by the charmless sight of Didcot Power Station billowing out its clouds on your left.

You have a choice of turning right into Green Lane after about half a mile which will bring you out into Bayworth or following the road round to Sunningwell.

Sunningwell

The Church Tower in this attractive little village was used by Roger Bacon, the 13th century scientist and philosopher to assist in his astronomical observations. Another notary here was a 17th century dispenser of charity with the delightful name of Hannibal Baskerville. Baskerville brought down the wrath of his neighbours by extending his charity to building a barn to house itinerants. Unimpressed, the population of Sunningwell had him indicted at Abingdon for harbouring vagabonds.

Go through Sunningwell and turn right at the sign post to Bayworth next to the Flowing Well Pub. Follow the road until it turns left through the undistinguished hamlet of Bayworth and follow the sign to Boars Hill as the road bends to the left. There is now a steep climb up Foxcombe Hill which may reduce you to walking for about half a mile until you reach the give way sign. Turn left here to Boars Hill. Pass Warnborough College on your left and enjoy the views of hills and fields to your right. After about a quarter of a mile look out for the road on your right and the sign to Old Boars Hill and Youlbury.

Turn right here into Berkley Road and if you look right there is a fine view of Oxford City and a better one still to come.

Boars Hill

A wealthy residential area in the wooded Cumnor Hills, Boars Hill forms part of Oxford's Green Belt. Part of it was bought by the Oxford Preservation Trust in 1928 to ensure that the splendid views it has over the Oxford skyline would not be destroyed. The view was made immortal by the much over-quoted words of the Victorian poet Matthew Arnold in his poem "Thyrsis" where he refers to "that sweet City with her dreaming spires". Arnold made the area his home and his presence and poetry pervade the area. A short ride from Jarn Mound (see below) is Matthew Arnold's Field and Arnold drew much inspiration from the "Warm, green-muffled Cumnor Hills" (for further traces of Arnold's presence see Route 5). Other poets who have graced the area are John Masefield, Robert Graves and Robert Bridges who built what is now the Carmelite Priory near Youlbury in 1907.

Carry on past the homes of the affluent and past Foxcombe Hall (belonging to the Open University) to the next sign post indicating Jarn Mound.

Follow the sign and route to Jarn Mound which is set in a garden on your right.

Jarn Mound

This is an artificial hill built by Sir Arthur Evans, the archaeological explorer famous for his discoveries at Knossos. The Mound was completed in 1931 and the summit is 530ft above sea level. The Mound (built to preserve precious views of and around Oxford) provides extensive views of the city, the Vale of the White Horse, the Berkshire Downs, Wychwood Forest and the Chilterns. At the foot of the Mound Evans laid out a wild garden which provides a pleasant stopping point for a picnic.

From Jarn Mound turn immediately into Old Boars Hill and enjoy about a mile of descent through hills and fields. At the bottom turn right into the B4017 to Wooton.

After nearly two miles turn off right where the sign post indicates Cumnor Hill and avoiding the A420 ahead. Enjoy another long swoop down Cumnor Hill, through Botley Road which will bring you past the Railway Station and into the City.

Route 2:
Oxford – Shotover Plain – Wheatley – Waterperry – Worminghall – Stanton St John – Oxford

Distance: 20½ miles.

No real opportunities for cutting this short except by returning the way you came from Waterperry. You can extend the ride by proceeding North from Worminghall towards Oakley, Brill and Boarstall and returning via Horton-cum-Studley.

Map: Ordnance Survey Landranger 164.

Rail Access: The journey starts and finishes in Oxford.

Tourist Information: Oxford, St Aldates.

Cycle Shops: See appendix under Oxford Cycle Shops, no others on route.

Special Interest: Shotover, Waterperry Gardens.

Refreshments: Tea rooms at Waterperry (open all year), The Star Inn, Stanton St John.

General Description

This route takes in some of the quiet country lanes just east of Oxford. Although it begins with a long gradual climb to Headington followed by the steep rise up to Shotover Plain (see below) for the most part this is fairly flat terrain. The ride across Shotover is a bumpy track which can be muddy but is accessible to ordinary touring bikes. It makes a pleasant Sunday afternoon ride, the main stopping point being the beautiful garden centre at Waterperry (see below).

Route

Starting from Carfax Tower, follow the High Street to The Plain round-about and take the left-hand turn off into St Clements. Carry on to the first set of traffic lights opposite the large green hill of South Park on your right. Take the right-hand lane and turn right into Morrell Avenue which rises to a roundabout where you veer left into Warneford lane with the walled Warneford Hospital on your right. Follow the road to the second set of traffic lights at the junction with Windmill Road and carry straight over into Old Road.

Continue up Old Road, crossing the bridge over the A4142 and up towards Shotover. Time for low gears and half a mile of continuous climbing. Pass the sign post indicating Shotover Plain and Brasenose Woods. This is a narrow lane with trees which passes through a residential area. At the top, admire the view – you've earned it. There is a parking space here where cars must stop but you can cycle along the trackway past the field bordered by stones. You are on top of Shotover.

Shotover

Shotover forms part of the ring of hills around the Thames flood-plain in which Oxford lies. The name is probably derived from the old English phrase *Sceot ofer* meaning steep hill. The area was once an extensive royal forest serving as an exclusive hunting ground for the monarch. The grandfather of John Milton of "Paradise Lost" fame (see also Route 6 and 7 and Stanton St John for more Milton connections) was once a ranger here.

An apocryphal story tells how an Oxford student from Queen's College was attacked on Shotover by a wild boar. The student was reading Aristotle at the time and put his book to good use by ramming it down the boar's throat and killing it. The story is celebrated annually at Queens by the Boar's Head Feast (Aristotle has been replaced by an orange stuffed in the boar's mouth). Nowadays the area is deemed relatively safe and was designated a Country Park in 1980. Hard though it is to believe it, the bumpy track across the plain was once the main highway from Oxford to London.

Continue across Shotover until the path becomes paved again and begins a gentle descent through houses on your right and views over fields on your left. After about a mile of descent, the houses indicate that you are nearing an urban area. Follow the sign straight on to Wheatley and

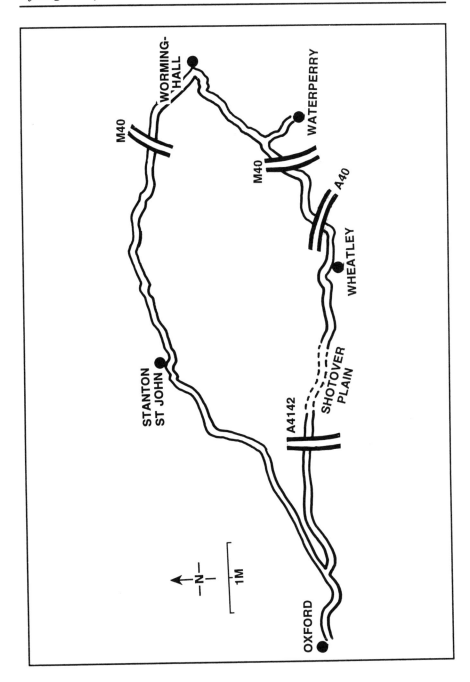

follow the road (with care!) as it narrows and bends to the right into Church Road, past the Sun Inn on your left.

Wheatley

Somewhere between a large village and a town, Wheatley has developed into a dormitory area for Oxford. It has a curious but not unpleasing mixture of the old and new with many Victorian buildings co-existing next to modern housing developments. The Victorian parish church of St Mary the Virgin has been rebuilt in thirteenth century style.

Carry on through Wheatley. At the end of Church Road, turn right to Waterperry and take the first turning on the left into Old London Road where there is a sign to Waterperry Gardens. After about a third of a mile turn left again, still following the sign to Waterperry. Pass under the bridge beneath the A40 after the Holton Village sign and go past Oxford Brookes University (formerly the Poly) Wheatley Campus on your left. From this point the urban recedes and the rural flat fields start to spread out before you.

Cross over the M40 and follow the road round to the right. The dead-end road will lead you through Waterperry to the Waterperry Gardens at the end.

Waterperry Gardens

Set in 83 acres around Waterperry House and describing itself as "a gardener's garden" Waterperry started as a horticultural centre in 1932. Today the centre is still used by Oxfordshire County for day release and amateur courses but it is open to visitors as a garden centre throughout the year. The showpiece is the Ornamental Gardens set by the River Thame (not to be confused with Thames) for which an entrance fee is charged. There is also a garden shop, a tea room and the Parish Church of Waterperry, St Mary the Virgin (another one) which lies in the walls of Waterperry House. The church contains original Jacobean pews, a three decker pulpit and ancient glass ranging over four centuries.

Leaving Waterperry Gardens and Waterperry, follow the road back through the village and take the first turn to the right to Worminghall. Follow the winding flat road through fields for just over a mile to the unremarkable village of Worminghall. Go through the village, following the road as it bends to the left. At the give way sign at the end of the village turn left into Menmarsh Road and follow the sign telling you that Stanton St John is four miles away.

Follow the road and cross over the M40 (again) and pass the eerily named Hell Coppice on your right and Waterperry Common on your left. At the next junction turn left to Oxford and Stanton St John.

Stanton St John

This pretty and largely unspoilt village was home to John Milton's grandfather (the Shotover Forest ranger). The village's other claim to fame is as the birth place of John White (born in 1575) who founded the Pilgrim Fathers. His former house is just opposite the church.

Follow the road through Stanton St John past, the parish church on your left and then veer round to the right and straight on to the junction with the B4027. Dog-leg right then immediately left where the sign indicates Headington (two and a half miles) and Oxford (five). Follow the road against the backdrop of hills and the sight of Barton Housing Estate in the distance. At the junction turn left and follow the road as it swoops down before rising up through Barton to the ultra busy Green Road Roundabout. Either negotiate with extreme care or plot your way through the confusing subway (probably the lesser evil) until you turn right in London Road. Follow London Road back down through Headington, down the steep hill, past the traffic lights and back the way you came to Carfax.

Route 3:
Oxford – Woodstock – Bladon – Yarnton – Oxford

Distance: 21 miles.

The route can be shortened by about three miles by missing out the visit to Bladon and returning via the original cycle path to Woodstock.

As this is a thematic trail, there is no obvious extension to the route but the ride can be continued by carrying straight on from Bladon to Long Hanborough and returning via Eynsham.

Map: Ordnance Survey Landranger 164.

Rail Access: The journey starts and finishes in Oxford.

Tourist Information: Hensington Road, Woodstock, and Oxford, St Aldates.

Cycle Shops: Woodstock Bike Shed, 1 Shipton Road, Woodstock, and see appendix under Oxford Cycle Shops.

Special Interest: Blenheim Palace, Oxfordshire County Museum and Winston Churchill's burial place.

Refreshments: Tea rooms, restaurants and pubs in Woodstock, Tea Rooms at Blenheim Palace. Picnics can be eaten in the grounds of Blenheim Palace or in the gardens of Oxfordshire County Museum.

General Description

Part of the popular tourist trail, this route is suitable for cyclists thanks to the commuter cycle route stretching from north Oxford to Woodstock. The ride takes in the splendours of Blenheim Palace, birth place of Winston Churchill, and the pleasant town of Woodstock before returning along quiet country lanes via Bladon and Churchill's burial place. This is a fairly gentle ride with only mild undulations. The route is straightforward in spite of a generous sprinkling of roundabouts.

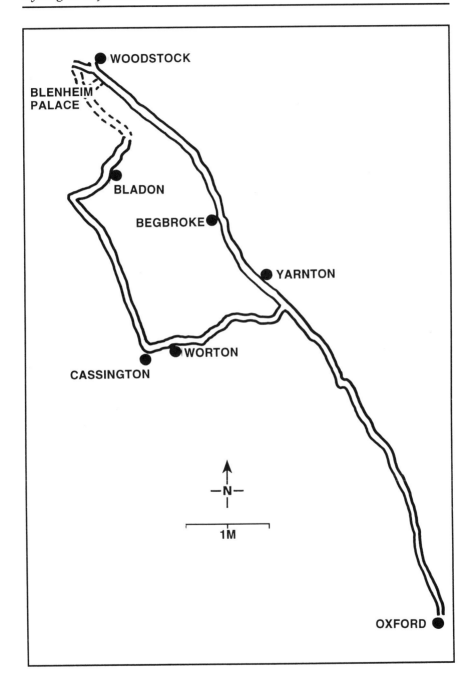

Route

From Carfax, wheel your bicycle up the pedestrianised Cornmarket street and take to two wheels from where it runs into Magdalen Street. Keep to the centre of the road and carry straight over the traffic lights by the Randolf Hotel at the junction with Beaumont Street. You now enter St Giles where you should stick to the left-hand cycle lane (as opposed to the one in the centre of the carriage way) and keep left as the road runs into Woodstock Road (A4144).

Follow the Woodstock Road through the affluent suburbs of North Oxford for about two miles. As you approach the end of the Woodstock Road you will see the beginning of the Woodstock Commuter Cycle Route which runs on the pavement to Woodstock. You can follow this straight over the Woodstock Road roundabout, dismounting at the intervening islands or cycle with the traffic, rejoining the cycle path which runs parallel to the A44. Cycle on between the hedgerow and the vicious-sounding traffic on your right to the huge Pear Tree roundabout which siphons off some of it. Cross over the roundabout via the cycle path to emerge on the other side (still on the A44). The worst is over.

On your left you should catch a glimpse of rolling woodland before this is obscured by hedgerows. Follow the meandering, slightly undulating path past more hedgerows and hints of fields to Yarnton roundabout and "The Grapes" pub on your right. Go straight over the roundabout, after which the cycle path temporarily disappears but you rejoin it again at Yarnton Post Office. The route continues through Begbroke through another roundabout (you can turn left here to visit the Norman Church of St Michaels, notable for its stained glass dating from the 16th century).

There are a few remaining miles to go to Woodstock, past Kidlington Airport on the right. As you approach Woodstock, the dry stone walling and trees indicate that your are on the outskirts of Blenheim Palace Estate. Enter Woodstock and a sign will tell you that Blenheim Palace is imminent and on your left you will catch a first glimpse through the main gate. The cycle path ends here and it's back to the road and the centre of Woodstock.

Woodstock

Lying eight miles north-west of Oxford on the edge of the Cotswold Hills, Woodstock is an attractive and prosperous town. Once a royal hunting ground (the name means "clearing in the woods"), the town is now notable for its well-preserved 18th century charm. It has the obligatory tea shops, antique shops and stocks in the main street but has managed to avoid the greater excesses of tourism and is a lived-in town rather than a showpiece. The Oxfordshire County Museum on Park Street is worth a visit (Admission free). The museum offers a fairly concise history of life in the county from the Ice-Age to the present and has displays of the Woodstock local trades of glove-making and steel. You are welcome to sit in the museum gardens which contain a number of permanent modern sculptures which could be described as 'interesting'. Bicycles are not allowed in the grounds.

Further down Park Street is Chaucer's House. The poet is known to have lived in Woodstock but the house is named after his son. (for more connections with Chaucer in the county see Route 9)

The stocks, Woodstock

Blenheim Palace

There are two entrances to the palace – the main one you passed on the way to Woodstock and another at the end of Park Street. Either way the view is magnificent. You can buy an all-inclusive ticket for the Palace and grounds or just visit the grounds. Cycling is not permitted except on the entrance and exit routes.

Home to the Dukes of Marlborough and designed by Vanbrugh, Blenheim is one of the most famous historic homes in Europe. This splendid Baroque affair was given to John Churchill, first Duke of Marlborough, for his military success at Blenheim in 1704. Home to the present Duke, the Palace itself covers over 7 acres. You may wonder as did the poet Alexander Pope "Tis very fine, but where d'ye sleep and where d'ye dine" but it rarely fails to impress. Guided tours are crisp and often witty and include the room where Winston Churchill was born.

The landscaped parkland (the work of Capability Brown) covers over 200 acres – quite a lot for one day but a very impressive backdrop for a picnic and a stroll over the man-made lake to the Victory Column.

Blenheim Palace

Leave Blenheim by following the exit route across the estate, past the narrow gauge estate minitrain, butterfly houses and fields of sheep. At the end turn right for Bladon into the A4095. Alternately, leave by the main gate, turn right and follow the road to the roundabout where you turn right to Bladon. Carry on for about a mile until you reach the village of Bladon. On your left, on top of a hill, you will see the parish church of St Martins where Winston Churchill is buried with other members of the Churchill family. Go up the hill to the church. The site is not signposted and the Churchill grave is a simple slab of stone. Other than its famous dead, the church remains very much a local parish church.

From the church continue through the unspoilt village of Bladon for half a mile. Turn left at the signpost to Cassington and follow the single-track road through rolling farmland and wooded hills. The odour can be distinctly farm-yardish and the fields provide an attractive patchwork of colour. This is a relatively straight road, crossing over the single railway track that links Oxford to the Cotswolds. Follow the road for about two and a half miles until the crossroad. Turn left here to Yarnton and Worton. After a mile or so you arrive in the small village of Yarnton with the Red Lion pub on your right. You could do a small detour here down Church Lane cul-de-sac to look at the small village church and the impressive exterior of Yarnton Manor.

Back in Yarnton carry on past the Pater Noster Farm shop on your right and rejoin the A44 at the roundabout at the end of the road. Turn right to return to Oxford rejoining the cycle path here and follow the route back into Oxford.

Route 4:
Oxford – Woodeaton – Islip – Charlton-on-Otmoor – Horton-cum-Studley – Beckley – Elsfield – Oxford

Distance: 25 miles.

No real opportunities for cutting this short as it follows a circular route around the moor. This route can be merged with Route 2 by continuing from Horton-cum-Studley to Worminghall and returning via Waterperry, Wheatley and Shotover.

Map: Landranger Ordnance Survey 164.

Rail Access: The journey starts and finishes in the centre of Oxford.

Tourist Information: Oxford, St Aldates.

Cycle Shops: See Appendix under Oxford Cycle Shops, on the route at Marston is Ivor Hall, 13 Old Marston Road, Marston, Oxford.

Special Interest: Otmoor.

Refreshments: The Swan at Islip, The Plough at Noke (not Mondays).

General Description

This route takes in the country north east of Oxford around Otmoor. Despite its proximity to Oxford, Otmoor has been described as the loneliest place in Oxfordshire and the Moor has acquired a special place in Oxfordshire folklore (see below). Flat and fenny, the area has more than its fair share of mist and rain so waterproofs are advisable for this route. Most of the route is low-lying with a few swoops and rises. There are a good number of pleasant views and sleepy villages (thatched cottages thrown in) but even on this quiet route there are traces of the rich and famous. Islip is the birth place of Edward the Confessor and Elsfield is the former home of the novelist John Buchan.

Otmoor

Otmoor means "Fen of Otta" and for centuries this 4000 acres of land was used for common grazing. Its wet, marshy nature and low lying terrain mean that even today the area requires large scale drainage for agriculture to be profitable. Drainage ditches are in evidence along the route and the area around Noke is the principle agricultural area.

The "Seven Towns" of Otmoor, as they are misleadingly called, are a collection of small villages forming a circle around the Moor. Beckley, Noke, Oddington, Charlton-on-Otmoor, Fencott, Murcott and Horton-cum-Studley had collective grazing rights on the Moor dating back to before the Middle Ages and regulated by the Lords of Beckley. Otmoor managed to resist the Enclosure of open fields movement until 1830 when the militia were called in to stop the moormen sabotaging the drainage and enclosure works. About 50 were arrested and brought to Oxford where they managed to escape amongst the crowds in St Giles's annual Fair. The crowds demonstrated their sympathy for the men by pelting the soldiers with stones and the prisoners were freed to the rallying cry of "Otmoor for Ever". Despite the rioting Enclosure had been largely completed by 1835 and many of the local poor lost their grazing rights and suffered hardship.

Otmoor remained as private grazing land until 1920 when it fell into the hands of the RAF and was used as a private bombing range. During the Second World War Otmoor was used as decoy airfield to distract German bombers.

The central area of Otmoor has been designated as a Site of Special Scientific Interest (it also contains a Ministry of Defence shooting range which, has protected the area from cultivation). As the wettest part of the Moor, the central area offers a habitat for wetland birds, flowers and insects and is a popular site for walkers.

Route

From Carfax follow the High Street to The Plain roundabout where you veer left into St Clements and carry onto the first set of traffic lights (opposite South Park and Morrell avenue). Stay in the left-hand lane and turn left into Marston Road (B4150) at the second set of traffic lights.

Carry on past the sprawling social security buildings on your right for just over a mile to the roundabout at the end of Marston Road where

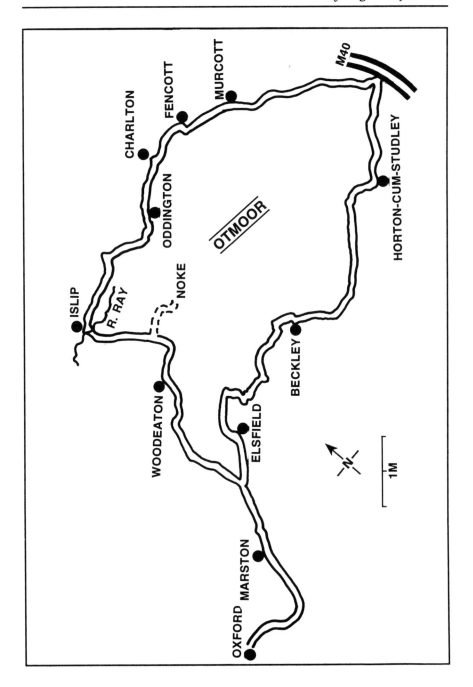

you will see the sign post for the Ring Road. Turn left here and right at the next Roundabout which follows very quickly into Marsh Lane. Carry on down Marsh Lane, crossing the bridge over the A40 and ignoring the slip road down to the Ring Road on your left. The road veers round to the left and you turn right following the sign to Elsfield. Be careful here of fast cars coming off the A40.

Take the first left, following the sign to Woodeaton (two miles). You now have a sense of leaving the urban behind as you follow the narrow lane through fairly flat fields to the village of Woodeaton. Like many local villages, Woodeaton is a mixture of the old and the new, but the parish Church of the Holy Rood on your right is definitely antiquated and well worth a visit. Dating back to the 13th century it is a simple little church but it can boast a medieval wall painting, a manorial pew and a minstrel's gallery.

Woodeaton Church

When you've seen it take a deep breath and follow the hill up through the village before making a gentle descent to the junction of the B4027 road where you turn left following the sign saying Islip one and three quarter miles. Set slightly off from the road is "The Plough Inn" at Noke on your right if you need refreshment at this stage. From this road you gain a first impression of Otmoor. Enjoy the extensive views to the right before a climb and a gentle descent takes you into Islip across a stone bridge over the River Ray.

Islip

Despite its small, sleepy appearance, Islip has had a notable past. King Ethelred had a palace here on the River Ray where his son Edward the Confessor was born in 1004. Edward subsequently gave the village to the Abbey at Westminster.

Situated on the old road from London to Worcester, Islip was the market centre for the Otmoor villages from the 14th to the 19th century.

Over the bridge of the River Ray you can turn right by the Swan Inn and follow Lower Street until it joins the road to Oddington. Turn right here and follow the road for about a mile and a half as it winds through flat lying fields. Look out for the signpost right to Oddington (and the Oxfordshire Cycleway sign) which takes you down a single track lane through the hamlet of Oddington. At the give way sign carry straight on and continue to Charlton-on-Otmoor about a mile away.

Charlton-on-Otmoor

An uncompromising mixture of the old and the new, Charlton is not the prettiest of villages but it does claim to have a good community spirit. The name means "free man's village" (whether it means free women as well is not known). The church is known, somewhat grandiosely, as the "Cathedral of Otmoor" and the bell has served as a guide for many a traveller lost in the mists on the Moor. It contains a rare pre-reformation Rood Screen which is decorated every May Day with a large cross of flowers.

From the end of the road in Charlton turn right to Fencott and Murcott and more views of Otmoor and pass Whitecross Green Wood on your right. Follow the steep hill towards the sounds of the M40. You'll know when you reach the top. Here you turn right to Horton-cum-Studley about two miles away. At Horton-cum-Studley take the road right, following the blue and white sign to Oxford and follow this road as it descends to the junction where you turn left to Beckley. Follow the road for about two miles before turning right into the attractive village of Beckley.

Beckley

Almost an archetypally pretty village, Beckley straddles the Roman route running from Alchester to Dorchester. The manor of Beckley has been through the hands of many powerful men including Edward the Second's favourite, Piers Gaveston. Beckley was also the scene for R.D. Blackmore's novel "Cripps the Carrier", published in 1877.

Follow the road as it winds through the village, veering left up hill. At the junction turn left past the church then dog-leg right into Common Road – a narrow lane which will bring you out on to the B4027 after about half a mile. Turn left into the B road and turn almost immediately right at the sign saying Elsfield one mile. Pass through farmland to the pretty, village of Elsfield.

Elsfield

Between 1919 and 1935 the novelist John Buchan (author of "The Thirty-Nine Steps") lived at the Manor House at Elsfield and wrote a number of books here. Buchan included local scenery in his work and "Midwinter" (published in 1923) contains scenes of Otmoor. He is buried in the church yard at Elsfield. (For further Buchan connections see Route 13 under Minster Lovell).

Go through Elsfield, following the road until it joins the B4150 again where you begin to see Oxford's urban sprawl and the large white edifice of the John Radcliffe Hospital. Here rejoin the road back to Marston, following the route you took earlier.

Route 5:
Oxford – Swinford – Stanton Harcourt – Bablock Hythe – Northmoor – Appleton – Cumnor – Oxford

Distance: 25 miles.

No real opportunities for cutting this short. You can merge this route with Route 1 by turning right to Bessels Leigh at Eaton. From Bessels Leigh go through Sandleigh into Old Boars Hill.

Map: Ordnance Survey Landranger 164.

Rail Access: The journey starts and finishes in Oxford.

Tourist Information: Oxford St Aldates.

Cycle Shops: See appendix under Oxford Cycle Shops and The Cycle and Sports Shop, 64 Mill Street Eynsham.

Special Interest: Swinford Toll Bridge, Pope's Tower and the Manor at Stanton Harcourt, Matthew Arnold's Bablock Hythe and Elizabethan scandal at Cumnor.

Refreshments: Ferryman Inn at Bablock Hythe, Bear and Ragged Staff at Cumnor.

General Description

This route follows quiet back roads west of Oxford. For the most part it is fairly flat with the backdrop of hills around Cumnor. It takes a swoop around the middle Thames, crossing the river over one of the two remaining Toll Bridges on the Thames and returning back over at Newbridge. Most of the route passes through farmland and wooded country lanes. There are a few poetic links with this route as it covers a region frequented by both Alexander Pope and Matthew Arnold.

Route

From Carfax wheel your bike through the pedestrianised Queen Street into New Road. Ride past the Prison on your left and into the one-way Park End Street. At the traffic lights at the end carry straight on, past the Railway station on the right, under the bridge and into Botley Road (A420). Cross Osney Bridge over the Thames and carry straight on for about one mile to the Traffic lights at "The Carpenters Arms". Carry straight on here under the bridge beneath the A34, past the Elms Parade shops on your left and turn right where the sign indicates Eynsham and the B4044 road and Farmoor Reservoir.

Follow the B4044 past houses and under the A420 bridge. The road now begins to wind through open farmland with a pleasant backdrop of hills and takes you to the small village of Farmoor. Cross straight over the roundabout and past the garage and shops on your left. Follow the road as it bends right then left towards Swinford Toll Bridge, crossing over the meandering Thames.

Swinford Toll Bridge

One of only two remaining toll bridges on the Thames (the other is at Whitchurch on the Oxfordshire/Berkshire border), Swinford Toll Bridge first came into operation in 1769. It was built by the fourth Earl of Abingdon to replace the dangerous ford crossing – John Wesley nearly drowned here on one of his many journeys through Oxfordshire. An 18th century Act of Parliament ensures that the cost is kept low – cars cross for the grand fee of 2p, but cyclists go free.

Over the bridge, cycle past "The Talbot" pub on your right to the roundabout where you turn left to the B4449 road and Stanton Harcourt. The next roundabout comes in rapid succession and you turn left again to Stanton Harcourt, by-passing the village of Eynsham, and carry on for two and a half miles.

Follow the road through flat farming landscape with distant hills in the background through Sutton and at the next roundabout turn left to Stanton Harcourt. The road takes you through the centre of the village with its modern village green (complete with playground) and winds round until you are opposite the Harcourt Arms Pub on your right and the parish church of St Michael (see below) on your left.

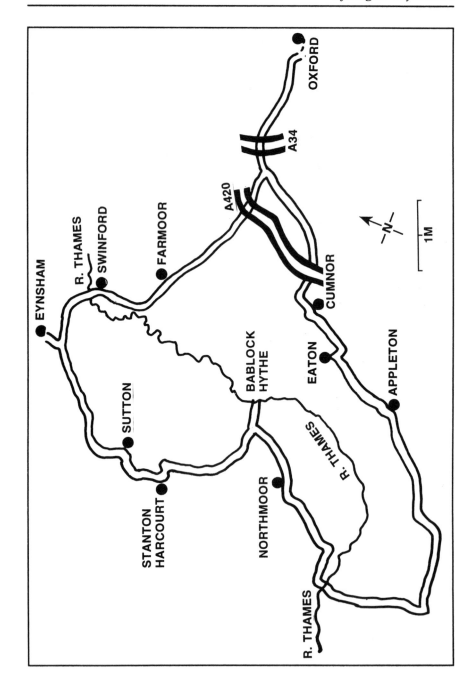

Carrying on along the road as it bends to the right you come to the entrance of Stanton Harcourt Manor on your left.

Stanton Harcourt and it Manor

The village dates back to Medieval times and the show piece is the intriguing Manor House complex built next to St Michael's Parish Church. Seat of the Harcourt family since the 12th century, much of the original Manor House was demolished in the 18th century when the family moved to nearby Nuneham Courtenay (see also Route 6) but two parts of special interest remain.

Pope's Tower

This is named after the poet Alexander Pope who translated the Iliad here between 1717 and 1718. He scratched the fact on a window pane to prove it – an act of vandalism which greatly enhances the tourist value.

The Great Kitchen

This was built in 1380 and is distinguished by its square tower, octagonal roof and the absence of a chimney (the smoke from the great ovens escaped through the louvres in the roof). According to Pope local people believed that witches kept their Sabbath here but there is little to substantiate this. The grounds of the manor have been transformed into a formal garden with fish ponds which make it a very pleasant place to visit.

Opening Times throughout the year are limited – check with tourist information or ring the Manor (0865) 881928

St Michaels Church

The church next to the Manor House dates back to Norman times and is in an unusually good state of preservation. It is a simple dignified little church and well worth a visit. Outside is a memorial stone to two lovers of local farm labouring families who were killed by lightening in 1718. Their epitaph was written by Pope who was deeply moved by the tragedy. Part of it goes:
"Victims so pure Heav'n saw well pleased
And snatched them in celestial fire"

You can read the rest on the outside wall of the church. Before you leave Stanton Harcourt there is another point of interest:

The Devil's Quoits

These are three upright prehistoric stones south of the village. Originally there were seven but the construction of an aerodrome in 1940 means that only three survive and two have been removed from their original place. There are two possible explanations for their presence – take your pick. The first is that they commemorate a Saxon victory. A more interesting though slightly less credible story is that they were thrown by the Devil while playing quoits for a beggar's soul. The story doesn't reveal who won the game.

From Stanton Harcourt follow the road for just under a mile to the crossroads and turn left into the single-track road to Bablock Hythe and Northmoor. Go past the hedgerows and fields of grazing sheep for a mile where you will see the sign to Bablock Hythe. make a short detour here by turning left, going past the mobile home park on your left until you reach the Thames and the Ferryman Inn at Bablock Hythe.

Bablock Hythe and Matthew Arnold

Found where the road meets the river, Bablock Hythe is an ancient ferry point which has been the site of an inn for centuries. Ferries were used to cross the Thames here for over 700 years and Bablock Hythe is commemorated by Matthew Arnold in the poem "The Scholar Gypsy" when he describes the hero:

"Crossing the stripling Thames at Bab-lock-hithe
Trailing in the cool stream thy fingers wet
As the punt's rope chops round"

Today you can sometimes get a lift over by a rowing boat but there are few provisions for cycles so you must turn back the way you came.

At the end of the road turn left to Northmoor and carry on down a quiet country lane for about a mile until you enter the tranquil village of Northmoor. At the end of the village turn left into Moreton Lane, following the signs to Newbridge and Kingston Bagpuize. Follow this narrow winding lane to the end which will bring you out with the Rose Renowned Inn and Restaurant on your left. Turn left here onto the A415 heading to Kingston Bagpuize. Cross over two Thames Bridges both with traffic lights and separated only by the Maybush Pub in the middle.

The road becomes hillier now and after some climbing take the left turn at the signpost to Appleton and Cumnor. After more gentle climbing you reach a plateau which takes you through the village of Appleton complete with duck pond and war memorial. Continue past the war memorial following the signs to Eaton and Cumnor and Oxford. At the next junction follow the road round to the right and left following the flattish road to Cumnor.

Cumnor

The ancient Manor of Cumnor, later known as Cumnor Place, was reputedly haunted by the ghost of Amy Robsart. Married to Robert Dudley, Earl of Leicester, Amy was found dead, possibly murdered, at a time when all the servants had been sent away for the day. Suspicion arose because Elizabeth 1 is said to have wanted to marry Dudley. The story was taken up and embroidered by Walter Scott in "Kenilworth".

The house which stood west of the church was demolished in 1810. A fine statue of Elizabeth and references to the Robsart saga can be found in the church.

At Cumnor, go past the large duck pond and turn right to Oxford at the junction. Keeping to the left, follow the one-way road to the end and stay left, crossing the bridge over the A420. At the give way sign turn left into Cumnor Hill and enjoy the long cruise downhill rejoining the route where you turned off towards Farmoor and carry straight on up Botley Road and back to Oxford city centre.

Route 6:
Oxford – The Baldons – Nuneham Courtenay – The Hamptons – The Haseleys – Great Milton – Cuddesdon – Garsington – Oxford

Distance: 27 miles.

Several opportunities for cutting this short – You can return to Oxford via the B480 at Chiselhampton. You can also reduce the journey by avoiding the Haseleys and Great Milton and going through Little Milton to Cuddesdon. You can also by-pass the Baldons and carry straight on to Chiselhampton and Stadhampton.

There are several opportunities to lengthen the route – you can carry on from Stadhampton to Chalgrove and link up with Route 7

From Great Milton you can return via Wheatley, linking with Route 2.

Map: Ordnance Survey Landranger 164.

Rail Access: The journey starts and finishes in the centre of Oxford.

Tourist Information: Oxford, St Aldates.

Cycle Shops: See Appendix under Oxford Cycle Shops.

Special Interest: Nuneham Courtenay Park, Garsington Manor Gardens, A famous restaurant and the birth place of John Milton (see Great Milton).

Refreshments: The Seven Stars Marsh Baldon, The Coach and Horses at Chiselhampton and, if you're feeling rich, Le Manoir aux Quat' Saisons at Great Milton.

General Description

This route takes in some of the small villages in the low-lying land just south-east of Oxford. Although it involves an initial trek through the now demolished site of the Cowley Rover Works (formerly Morris Motor Works) and the Blackbird Leys housing estate, the route rapidly gains a more rural feel as you enter arable land with wooded hills in the distance. The route goes through a number of small villages of which the prettiest are, arguably, Little Haseley and Great Milton (plenty of thatch and wood smoke) and despite always being within reasonable distance of the City, the area feels genuinely rural. The majority of the ride is fairly flat on easy-going terrain with a moderate rise up to Toot Baldon and a fairly steep one to Cuddesdon and Garsington. There are, of course, compensatory "down hills" too.

Route

From Carfax Tower proceed through the High Street to The Plain roundabout. Cross over the roundabout taking the second turn off left into Cowley Road (B480). Follow this road for about two miles until the traffic lights by the church at the top of the small hill. Carry straight over into Garsington Road and straight on across roundabouts and through traffic lights. Proceed with care (still on the B480) through the industrial complex and the Blackbird Leys estate on your right. After the housing estate the scenery opens up into arable farm land and wooded hills. Carry straight on, following the signs to Stadhampton and look out for a sign on your left pointing to The Baldons. Turn right into a single track road closed to motor vehicles (except access). Follow the lane as it rises through fields for about half a mile to Toot Baldon and the Crown Inn. From here follow the road as it winds towards Marsh Baldon.

The Baldons

Baldon refers to "Bealda's Hill". Toot indicates a single hill serving as a look-out point. Marsh Baldon is built around one of the most extensive village greens in the country and is on the course of the Roman road which cuts through here, running from Dorchester across Otmoor to Alchester just outside Bicester. The Church of St Peter at the end of Marsh Baldon is mainly 14th century but the sundial over the south of the door may date back to Saxon times.

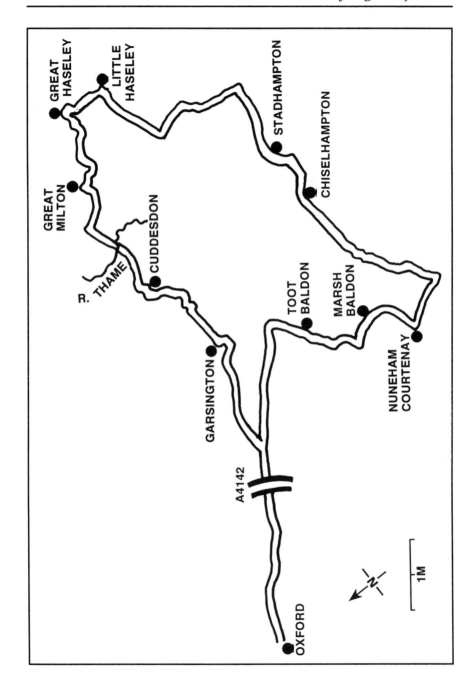

Go through Marsh Baldon, past the outsize village green and the Seven Stars Pub (serves food), past the Church and Baldon House and the road will bring you out through woodland onto the busy A423. To your right you will catch a glimpse of the red brick alms houses of Nuneham Courtney but you turn left following the sign to Reading. This road is BUSY so proceed with caution. About 350 yards on the right is the entrance to Nuneham Courtenay Park.

Nuneham Courtenay and Nuneham Park

The village of Nuneham Courtenay was built in the 1760s and is a recreation of the old village of Nuneham. The story goes that the first Earl of Harcourt took exception to the view of his tenants' miserable accommodation which he could see through the windows of Nuneham House and ordered a wholesale relocation. The poet Oliver Goldsmith is believed to be referring to Nuneham in the poem "The Deserted Village" when he refers to :

"The man of wealth and pride
Takes up a space that many poor supplied"

The Harcourts are of the same ilk as those from Stanton Harcourt (Route 5). The first Earl's grandfather took over the Nuneham estate in 1710. The house is now owned by Oxford University and is used as a conference centre. The park, landscaped in the 18th century by Capability Brown (see also Blenheim Palace Gardens Route 3) is also owned by the University but can be visited.

From the park turn right, back into the A423 and proceed with care for about three quarters of a mile to the interestingly named Golden Balls roundabout. Turn left here following the sign to Stadhampton. This brings you into the B4015 road. Follow the road for just over two miles, passing Little Baldon Farm on your left, to the end of the road at Chiselhampton which brings you opposite The Coach and Horses 16th century Inn and Restaurant. (You can cut the journey short by turning left back to Oxford here – about seven miles).

Turn right into the B480 again and after about a mile turn left into the village of Stadhampton by the Post Office and Gibbs Garage. Go past the large village green on your right. Turn right at the small roundabout following the sign to Chalgrove. You now have a fairly flat ride for about a mile to the sign indicating Rofford half a mile and Little Milton two. Turn left here and after just under two miles you will smell the "aroma" of Ditchend pig farm. Just after the farm turn right into the single track road to Little and Great Haseley. Enjoy the receding smell. After a mile you reach the rural idyll of Little Haseley where the road veers to the left and after half a mile left again into Great Haseley.

The Haseleys

These two attractive villages take their name from "hazel wood". They are unspoilt and have an aura of peace and timelessness about them. The father of architect Christopher Wren lived at the rectory at Great Haseley and was dean of Westminster.

From Great Haseley turn left at the sign in the middle of the village to Great Milton one and a half miles. Note the Windmill on your right as you cycle the half mile to the A329. Turn left here at the sign to Wallingford and first right to Great Milton and Great Milton Manor. About 500 yards up the road on your right you will see the wrought iron gates of Le Manoir aux Quat' Saisons, owned and presided over by master chef Raymond Blanc. You can stop off for a meal or pass on through the village and past the church on your right.

Great Milton

Another highly attractive village, complete with village green, cottages and substantial houses, Great Milton's claim to fame (other than its illustrious restaurant) is that John Milton author of "Paradise Lost" is believed to have originated from here (his grandfather was a ranger at Shotover Forest – see Route 2 and 7). No one quite knows which was the Milton family house but it is thought to be one of the gabled ones in Jacobean style near the church. There is a rumour that Milton wrote Paradise Lost here but this has not yet been substantiated.

From Great Milton take the left turn off to Cuddesdon two miles. This single track road leads you up through sheep grazing fields for about half a mile. At the top turn right, following the sign to Wheatley and after about 500 yards turn left into a gentle descent which will bring you across the stone and wrought iron bridge across the River Thame (not the Thames) and past Cuddesdon Water Mill.

The road veers slightly to the right before beginning an ascent of about one mile into the village of Cuddesdon. The views from the Church are exceptional, taking in the Chilterns and Berkshire Downs across the valley of the River Thame. Go through the village and at the junction by the village green turn left following the signs to Garsington one and a half miles. Take the fairly rapid descent through the hamlet of Denton and turn right then shortly after left to begin an ascent into Garsington. After about a mile the road ends opposite a school. Turn left here at the sign to Oxford and Cowley. Follow the road as it descends to the left and right through the village but first pay a visit to Garsington Manor gardens.

Garsington Manor

The manor lies south of the church, slightly down the hill. You can only visit the gardens but they are well worth it. Designed by Lady Ottoline Morrell between 1915 and 1924, they are Italianate in style with monastic fish ponds, a water garden and a 17th century dovecote. The 16th century manor house has seen some notable guests and Lady Ottoline is best known as a hostess to assorted members of the Literati. Names which have graced the building include Siegfried Sassoon, Bertrand Russell, Aldous Huxley, Virginia Woolf, Lytton Strachey, Katherine Mansfield and D.H. Lawrence. There has been recent speculation that Ottoline may have been the prototype for Lawrence's Lady Chatterley (see "Ottoline" by Miranda Seymour, Sceptre).

From Garsington you should gain your first glimpse of Oxford's urban sprawl. Follow the road and signs to Oxford for about two miles past the village of Blenheim (not **the** Blenheim) until it rejoins the B480 leading into Cowley Road. Turn right here and follow the road back to the Town Centre.

Route 7:
Oxford – Stanton St John – Shabbington – Thame – Chalgrove – Little Milton – Wheately – Shotover – Oxford

Distance: 38 miles.

Not many opportunities for cutting short, except returning from Thame via the A418. The route can be linked with Route 6 and Route 2 to lengthen.

Map: Ordnance Survey Landranger 164 and 165.

Rail Access: The journey starts and finishes in Oxford.

Tourist Information: Thame, Town Hall, High Street.

Cycle Shops: Thame Cycles, 69a Park Street, Thame.

Special Interest: Chalgrove Monument, Shotover.

Refreshments: The Star Inn Stanton St John, several pubs, cafes and restaurants in Thame selling food.

General Description

This route passes through the low-lying farmland in East Oxfordshire, close to the Buckinghamshire border. Although quite a long ride, it is for the most part easy cycling but there are a number of hills after Thame. As with most hills however, the views are correspondingly enhanced in particular looking to the south over the Chiltern Hills. The final part of the journey from Wheatley to Shotover involves a long rise to Shotover plain. The route across the plain can be adequately negotiated by an ordinary tourer although it is sometimes muddy. The final part is a long descent down the other side of Shotover and back into Oxford.

Route

From Carfax proceed along the High Street to the Plain roundabout where you take the left-hand turn off into St Clements. Proceed until the traffic lights by South Park. Continue straight on through both sets and up the hill of London Road, through the shops at Headington until the busy Green Road roundabout at the end (about three miles in total).

Either use the subway or negotiate the roundabout with great care to turn off at the second road on your left (Bayswater Road). From here follow the signs to Stanton St John. After a long swoop and what feels like a longer rise look for the sign to turn right to Stanton St John.

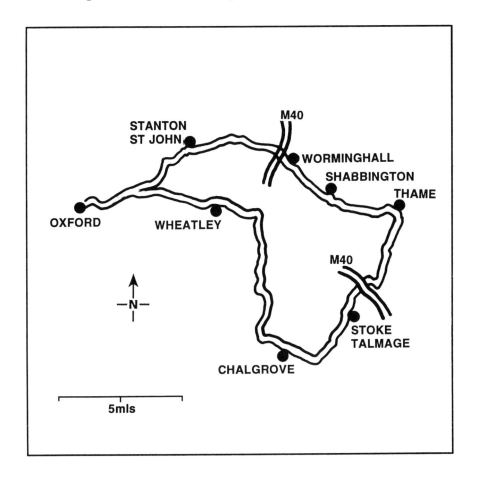

Follow this quiet country road for about one mile to the end then dog leg right and left into Stanton St John (See ride 2).

Follow the road through the village and between Holly Wood on your left and Stanton Great Wood on your right (if you're lucky you may see a deer). After about one and a half miles you reach the locally known Menmarsh Guide Post. Turn right here following the sign to Worminghall and Thame. Pass by Hell Coppice on your left and Waterperry Wood on your right.

Follow the road as it slips temporarily over the border into Buckinghamshire, crossing over the M40 to the villages of Worminghall, Ickford and Shabbington where the route veers right towards Thame. Just beyond Shabbington cross over the River Thame (sometimes in danger of flooding here) and follow the road to the end at the junction with the A418. Turn left here and follow the A418 for about one mile until it brings you to a roundabout where you follow the signs to the town centre, of Thame.

Thame

Thame is a pleasant market town whose broad and seemingly endless High Street is lined with 18th century houses. The 13th century church of St Mary the Virgin contains some impressive monuments to the noble dead and the Lord William school on Church Road boasts John Milton and John Hampden (see under Chalgrove) as former pupils. John Hampden, the Civil War Hero, died here of wounds received at the Battle of Chalgrove Field (1643) and is commemorated by a plaque on a site near the Victorian town hall. Also worth a visit here is the working forge on the High Street – ironware rather than horses but you're welcome to browse in this link with the past.

When you've finished with Thame proceed through High Street and look out for the sign off to the right to Postcombe down Thame Park Road. Turn right through the industrial estate until you join the B4012. On your left pass by Thame Park on the site of the Cistercian Thame Abbey. The Abbey has been incorporated into a private house.

You now come into open fields and rising hills (look left for a first glimpse of the Chiltern Hills). Follow the road until it joins the A40 where you turn right at the sign to Tetsworth and run parallel to the

M40. Just past Attington stud farm on your right turn left, going under the M40 towards Stoke Talmage. Follow this road as it gently, then more steeply rises past the hamlet of Stoke Talmage followed by Clare and Golder. Stoke Talmage lies at the foot of the Chiltern escarpment and is a small agricultural settlement with a tiny population. Further up the hill Clare and Golder are two of the county's deserted villages – not even designated hamlets. Climb up to the top of Clare Hill. Enjoy the views and the descent to Cutt Mill.

Turn right here onto the B480 to Chalgrove. After two miles of fairly flat cycling pass by Chalgrove and spare a moment for the Hampden memorial found a little way down the road on the right.

Chalgrove

Although fairly unremarkable today, Chalgrove has had a notable past. During the Civil War the battle of Chalgrove Field was fought in 1643. The outcome was a royalist victory for Prince Rupert and the death of the celebrated Parliamentarian John Hampden who is commemorated here by a fairly unimpressive monument erected here in the 19th century on Chalgrove field.

Carry on past the huge expanse of Chalgrove Airfield on your right and after about one and a half miles look for the sign right to Rofford and Little Milton. Turn right here for more flat cycling for about two miles to the attractive village of Little Milton. Follow the road as it forks to the right and at the end turn right into the A329 before taking the first turn left to Wheatley (four miles) and Oxford (ten). Follow the road to the end where it veers to the left and continue following the signs to Wheatley. After about three miles go under the old railway bridge and turn left at the sign to Wheatley. Ride into Wheately for about one mile before turning left at the Kings Arms into Church Street.

Follow the road through the village with care at the narrow twisting descent. After the village begin the long slow rise to Shotover and across Shotover Plain.

See ride 2 for details of Shotover and Wheatley.

From Shotover go down the sharp descent, over the A4142 ring road. Carry on through Headington Old Road to the traffic lights at the junction of Windmill Road. Go straight over and, descending, go through the traffic lights, past the Warneford Hospital on your left and South Park on your right. At the roundabout turn right into Morrell Avenue, descend to the traffic lights at the end where you turn left to follow the road back into the town centre.

ROUTES 8 – 10

The Chilterns and the Thames Valley

The Chilterns comprise a beautiful landscape of farmland, chalk hills, woodlands and downland. The chalk hills for which the area is famous cover a total area of 800 square kilometres and as well as falling in the southern tip of Oxfordshire they extend into Bedfordshire, Buckinghamshire and Hertfordshire.

In 1965 the Chilterns were designated an Area of Outstanding Natural Beauty and they provide a spectacular backdrop for the rides in this section. Areas of chalk downland support rich and increasingly rare plant communities including the elusive pasque flower and Chiltern gentian. Many areas of chalk downland are Sites of Special Scientific Interest and the area around Aston Rowant is a National Nature Reserve.

As well as the chalk hills, the Chilterns are renowned for the famous beechwoods of the region. Once used to supply London firewood, the forests became a valuable source of raw material for the furniture industry in the 17th century. They also provided a home for the "bodgers" – local craftsmen who lived and worked in the woods until modern machinery superseded handicrafts. Today the forests are home to woodland flora and the wildlife includes the greater spotted woodpecker, fallow and muntjac deer and the introduced edible dormouse.

There is evidence of human settlement in the Chilterns from pre-iron age and the area exudes a sense of prehistoric mystique. The ancient trading and pathways of the Icknield Way, Swan's Way and the Ridgeway cross through this part of Oxfordshire and the Romans farmed the fertile soil of the valleys draining south towards the Thames. A noticeable feature of this area is the flinty soil in the valley slopes. A man-made feature seen frequently in the villages is the wells built to counteract the difficulty in obtaining a constant water supply in the Chiltern villages in the past. Many of the wells sink deep into the hills – some over 350ft.

The Thames Valley

From just above Goring to just above Henley the River Thames forms a natural border between Oxfordshire and Berkshire. This is a particularly beautiful stretch of the river with the Thames meandering against the backdrop of the Chiltern Hills. At Goring, the Berkshire Downs, the Chiltern Hills and the Ridgeway path all converge and this is a very popular stretch for boaters, forming the heart of the Thames Valley.

Route 8:
Goring – North Stoke – Ipsden – Well Place – Stoke Row – Woodcote – Goring

Distance: 17 miles.

The route can be shortened by about two miles by leaving Stoke Row to Checkendon and therefore omitting Ipsden Wood The route can be lengthened by merging with Route 10 and continuing from Stoke Row to Henley.

Map: Ordnance Survey Landranger 175.

Rail Access: The journey starts and finishes from Goring Station.

Tourist Information: None on route.

Cycle Shops: None on route.

Special Interest: Well Place Zoo and the Maharaja's Well at Stoke Row.

Refreshments: Pubs and a village store at Stoke Row. Several pubs and food shops on route.

General Description

Although this is the shortest of the three routes around the Chilterns it is arguably the prettiest. Passing through sparse chalk downland and ancient beechwoods, the landscape seems to breathe its ancient history – an impression enhanced by the numerous flints in low lying plough fields stretching up to the rolling downs. Inevitably there are hills, but for the most part the journey consists of gentle rising and falling and only the steep hill up Berinshill Wood can be described as truly challenging. The return part of the journey is enhanced by a constant gentle descent through Ipsden and Borocourt Wood and finishes on a long glorious roll downhill through more woodland to Cleeve and Goring.

Route

From Goring Station turn left into the B4009, passing through the village
and running parallel to the railway line. This is a straight run of about
three and a half miles of gently rising road to North Stoke. You pass
between arable fields (note the flints) set against a backdrop of hills.

At North Stoke (not to be confused with South, Little Stoke or Stoke
Row) turn right, following the sign that says Stoke Row five miles and
has a parrot's head sign for Well Place Zoo, two and a half miles. This is
a single track route taking you through another backdrop of hills. Cross
straight over at the junction with the A4074 with care and the road will
take you through stunning scenery to the village church of St Mary's at
Ipsden on your left.

Ipsden

Set in idyllic countryside, Ipsden was the home of the Victorian playwrite
Charles Reade whose father was the local squire and whose best known work
"The Cloister and the Hearth" was published in 1861.

Just outside the church is another mention of the Reade family inscribed on a
well – a gift from India installed here under the instructions of Michael Reade –
this is a forerunner of the well you will see in Stoke Row.

About half a mile from the church through yet more glorious scenery
you will begin to hear a cacophony of bird song and the parrot's head
will reveal its function. This is Well Place Zoo. If it agrees with your
principles pay a visit. It has a wide ranging collection of animals from
llamas to guinea pigs and a world wide collection of birds – if you don't
mind seeing them caged.

After the zoo the road veers to the right and there is the big climb of the
day – a fairly sharp and long climb up Berins Hill and through Berinshill
Wood to the give way sign near Ipsden Heath. At the give way sign turn
right and the road brings you into the main street of the village of Stoke
Row. As you ride through you will see the dome of the Maharajah's
Well on your left.

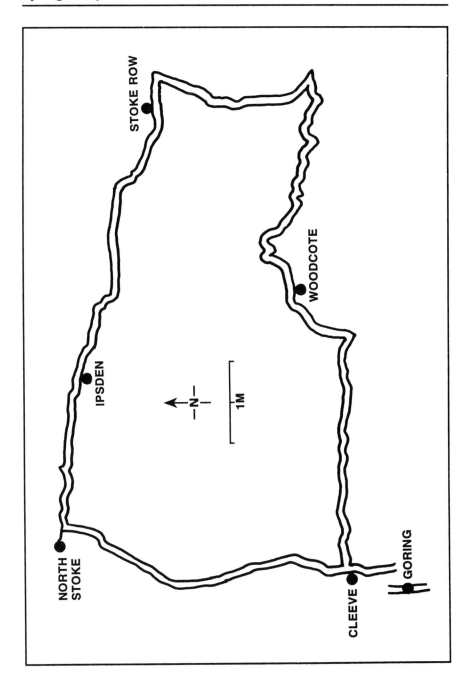

The Maharajah's Well

Maharajah's Well

This is a charming link with a not so charming past. The well was donated to the village of Stoke Row by the Maharaja of Benares in 1864 as a result of a conversation with Edward Reade from Ipsden. Reade described to the Maharajah the difficulties of obtaining water in Stoke Row and the Maharajah donated the well as a token of friendship and loyalty towards England. The ornate superstructure of the well has a distinctly oriental appearance complete with golden elephant. The well has been lovingly restored and repaired. It is a remarkable piece of engineering going down 368ft into the chalk land. Thankfully the Well Trustees have preserved it as a link with the past so it has not degenerated into a twee wishing well.

You can't drink your fill here but when you've had enough anyway proceed on through the village main street to the first main turning on your right opposite "The Farmers Inn" at the sign for the Business Park. Don't be put off by the sign – the route is much more promising than it sounds and takes you on a long descent through Basset Wood and Ipsden Wood leading into Borocourt Wood. These form part of the Chiltern Forest District.

Carry on descending until after about two miles you reach an unsignposted crossroad (this could change!) where you turn right. The following section of the route is not sign posted so refer to a map. Follow the route through more forest at Nippers Grove. The road veers round to the right past Rumerhedge Wood on your right then you turn right towards Checkendon. Take the first turning on your left which will take you through Cock's Hill. At the end of the road turn right into Exlade Street (yes, it is a street rather than a village), past the Highway Man Pub on your left. At the end of the road turn left following the sign to Woodcote. After about 500 yards this brings you to the busy A4074 where you dog leg right then left following the Oxfordshire Cycleway and Woodcote signs.

The road takes you through the village of Woodcote to the crossroads and war memorial where you turn left following the signs for Goring three and a quarter miles. This is the B471 which you follow for about half a mile to the bottom dip in the hill. At the base of the dip turn right following the signpost to Cleeve and South Stoke. Enjoy nearly two miles of long descent through the woodland of Elmorepark Wood on your right and Park Wood on your left, to the bottom of the hill where you turn left past Goring Service Station and follow the road back through Goring to the railway station.

Route 9:
Cholsey – Wallingford – Swan's Way – Stonor – Russell's Water Common – Nuffield – Wallingford – Cholsey

Distance: 28 miles.

Several opportunities to cut this route short – one possibility is to by-pass Nuffield by turning right on the B491 at Cookley Green and follow the minor road back to Crowmarsh Gifford and Wallingford Also several ways of lengthening the route – from Swan's Way you could continue on to the Ridgeway and turn right to Christmas Common rejoining the main route at the B480

From Ewelme you could carry on to Watlington, proceed to Christmas Common and rejoin the route as above.

Map: All the route except for the distance between Cholsey and Wallingford is on the Ordnance Survey Landranger 175. The route from Cholsey to Wallingford is well sign-posted and can be found on Ordnance Survey Landranger 174.

Rail Access: The journey starts and finishes at Cholsey Station.

Tourist Information: Wallingford, 9 St Martins Street.

Cycle Shops: Castles, St Mary's Street, Wallingford.

Special Interest: There are several graves of the famous on this route including Agatha Christie at Cholsey and Jerome K. Jerome, author of "Three Men in a Boat", at Ewelme where relatives of Chaucer are also buried. Also of interest is Wallingford Museum and Castle, and Stonor Park.

Refreshments: Tea shops, restaurants and pubs in Wallingford; tea shop at Stonor.

General Description

Not for the faint-hearted, this route has a fair number of ups and downs but there is the compensation of spectacular scenery in places. It begins through low-lying fields and farmland around Cholsey and later rises through the Chiltern Hills. In places there is a dramatic scenic backdrop of sparse hills and chalk downland as well as forest area and the extensive Maidensgrove and Russell's Water Common. The route also has the more urban attractions of the market town of Wallingford (see below) and the regal beauty and deer park of Stonor Estate. At Ewelme spare a few moments for the churchyard to look for famous names.

Route

Turn left out of Cholsey Station and follow the road through the village as it veers to the left. Cholsey doesn't have many claims to fame but the novelist Agatha Christie lived here for a time and she is buried with her archaeologist husband in the parish church. As the road winds round to the left look out for the signs to Wallingford. After just under two miles you reach a busy roundabout. Cross straight over where you will see a pedestrian and cycle path (this is not accessible to traffic). Follow this route for about 500 yards to the give way sign where you turn left, joining the A329 at Winterbrook. Follow the road for three quarters of a mile to Wallingford. As you approach the town centre veer left on the one-way system which brings you into St Martins Street and the town centre.

Wallingford

An attractive market town built on the River Thames, Wallingford is a popular tourist spot and has the antique and tea shops to prove it. The remains of a medieval castle are situated behind the George Hotel. The castle was destroyed in the Civil War (Wallingford was the last stronghold in the county to surrender to Cromwell) and the Castle site has been designated an Ancient Monument with parts of the ramparts and ditches remaining. The Wallingford Museum in High Street relates the town's history from Saxon to present times and includes information about the Castle.

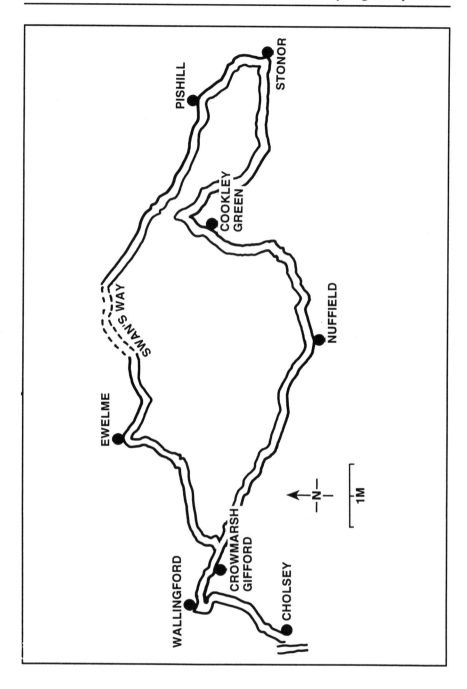

Another point of interest in Wallingford is that it is sited on the place where William the Conqueror finally crossed the River Thames. Parts of the beautiful seventeen arched bridge in Wallingford date back to Medieval times.

Leave Wallingford turning right at the traffic lights at the bottom of St Martins Street This brings you into the High Street leading to traffic lights before the bridge over the Thames. Cross the bridge and you will almost immediately enter the village of Crowmarsh Gifford and see more antique shops. Carry on straight over the first small roundabout until the second larger one where you take the second turn off left into Clacks Lane leading to Ewelme and RAF Benson.

You now begin a persistent gentle rise through farmland for about one and a half miles. The urban recedes but you may find the peace shattered by aircraft from nearby RAF Benson. At the give way sign dog leg right then left and left again to Ewelme about half a mile away.

Ewelme

In this attractive little village a chalk stream rises which flows down to the Thames near Benson and is the source for the well-known Ewelme watercress beds. The village church, almshouses and school all date back to the fifteenth century. In the Church are monuments of the Chaucer family (relatives of the more famous Geoffery) and outside in the churchyard is the grave of Jerome K. Jerome, author of "Three Men in a Boat".

From Ewelme follow the road back in a south easterly direction for about one third of a mile to the junction where you turn left and begin to rise through sparse dramatic hills of the Chilterns. After nearly one mile take the turn off straight ahead of you (the main road veers to the right) into Swan's Way. NB keep an eye open for it as it is not immediately obvious.

NOTE an alternative route in the event of bad weather or to reduce the miles is to follow the road on to Cookley Green and pick up the rest of the route on the B481 leading to the B480.

Swan's Way

This is a long-distance bridleway (65 miles) from Goring to Salcey Forest in Northants which coincides with the Ridgeway in parts.

The route ascends and descends through this bridlepath (which can be muddy in parts and is certainly very flinty) for about one and a half miles. At the end turn right into a long ascent up Britwell Hill. Congratulate yourself if you get to the top without walking and congratulate yourself even if you do walk – your reward is near. At the top cycle across the plateau through woodland and farmland for about one mile until the end of the road. Here turn right before turning swiftly left into the B480, following the signs to Stonor Park three miles and Pishill two miles.

Here you begin the long, long descent (well nearly two miles of it) through Pishill Bottom, Pishill Bank and Pishill hamlet. Follow the road as it veers round to the right taking you past Stonor Deer Park where you may see the deer.

Stonor Estate

Set within a secluded deer park, Stonor has been home to the Camoy famiy for over 800 years. It was built near the site of a prehistoric stone circle which has been reconstructed in the grounds.

The Stonors were a leading Catholic family and Edmund Campion, the Jesuit priest and martyr was given sanctuary here in the 16th century. There is a small museum dedicated to English Catholicism in the house. The house also contains rare items of furniture, drawings and paintings from Britain, Europe and the USA. Limited opening Times, telephone 0491 638587 for details.

As you enter the village of Stonor look out for the single track road on your right and the sign post to Maidensgrove and Russell's Water. Turn right here and begin ascending through woodland for about one mile to Maidensgrove and Russell's Water Common. The Common belongs to Stonor estate and cyclists should stick to the highway veering to the right across it. The Common forms a plateau across the surrounding Chiltern hills and provides beautiful views to the left across more hills.

After two miles you come to the junction of the B481. Turn left here following the signs to Nettlebed and passing through the small village of Cookley Green. The road is mainly descending for about one and a half miles. At the sign for Nuffield turn right. Follow this narrow road for about a mile before dog-legging right onto the A423 then left at the sign to Nuffield one mile. Go through Nuffield Common to the village of Nuffield where you turn right at the sign to Nuffield Church.

Nuffield

This was the chosen home of Lord Nuffield, formerly William Morris, founder of Oxford motor company (see under Oxford). He chose the name Nuffield after the Manor House here. His philanthropy means that the name of this humble village also graces an Oxford college and the Nuffield Hospital in Oxford.

Follow the road for another two miles of descending until the junction where you turn left into the A423, following the sign to Wallingford. After about one mile you reach the roundabout at Crowmarsh Gifford. Go straight over into the road rather unimaginatively named "The Street". This leads you back to the route taken previously through Wallingford to Cholsey.

Route 10:
Goring – Mapledurham – Henley-on-Thames – Stoke Row – Goring

Distance: 30 miles.

The distance can be shortened by about nine miles by going directly to Stoke Row from Gallowstree Common. The route can be lengthened by continuing from Henley to Stonor and joining Route 9.

Map: Ordnance Survey Landranger 175.

Rail Access: The journey starts and finishes at Goring Station.

Tourist Information: Town Hall, Market Place, Henley.

Cycle Shops: Hammonds, Bell Street, Henley.

Special Interest: Mapledurham House and Watermill, Grey's Court, The Maharaja's Well at Stoke Row.

Refreshments: Tea shop at Goring Heath Post Office; tea shops, restaurants and pubs at Henley. Several pubs *en route*.

General Description

Water seems to be a persistent theme for this route. Starting at Goring on the Thames the first half of the route runs close to the meanderings of the river. There is a watermill at Mapledurham – the last working one on the Thames – and Henley is famous for its annual boating Regatta. At Grey's Court is the last used donkey wheel for drawing water out of a well and the Maharaja's Well at Stoke Row brings us into contact with another water source of historical if not practical interest. Another places of historical interest is Mapledurham House near the watermill.

This route has its fair share of hills. For the most part it passes through alternating woodland, farmland and heath and this is one of the most beautiful sections of the Thames Valley.

Route

Turn left out of Goring Station and take the first road right by the Queen's Arms into the B4526. Follow the road on a long, moderately steep rise for nearly two miles before it flattens out around the small village of Cray's Pond. Carry straight on, following the signs to Reading. The road begins a gentle slope down hill through woodland and into open field.

After three and a half miles from Goring veer to the right, leaving the B road and follow the signpost indicating Goring Heath. Ride along the wooded road following the signs to Mapledurham, three and a quarter miles. At Goring Heath Post Office you can stop for tea at the tea room or carry straight on through more woodland and fields for about three miles until the crossroads and the sign post saying that Mapledurham House and Watermill are to your right. Turn right and go down the steep winding, narrow road (with care!) to Mapledurham at the bottom.

Mapledurham

This is a lovely secluded little village hidden from view on the Thames bank. Low red brick alms houses built in 1629 lead towards the 13th century parish church of St Margaret. On your right is Mapledurham Watermill and on your left, behind the church is the imposing facade of Mapledurham House

Return up the long hill to the crossroads and carry straight over, following the sign saying "Tinkers Green Only". This single track lane will bring you out on the busy A4074 after about a mile. Turn left here and dog leg right at the first right turn which is the narrow Mill Lane. Follow the series of steep descents and ascents through thick woodland and past the occasional house to the end (about half a mile). Turn left to Kidmore End. After half a mile you will reach the end of the road and the village well. Turn left and follow the road for one mile to the eerily named village of Gallowstree Common.

Here you can cut the journey short by dog legging right then left at the sign that says Stoke Row three miles or continue right, following the signs to Henley. Go through Gallowstree Common, Shiplake Bottom and the outskirts of Sonning Common to the crossroads and carry straight over still following the signs to Henley. Follow the short sharp hill descent then veer left onto the B481. Pass through Peppard Common

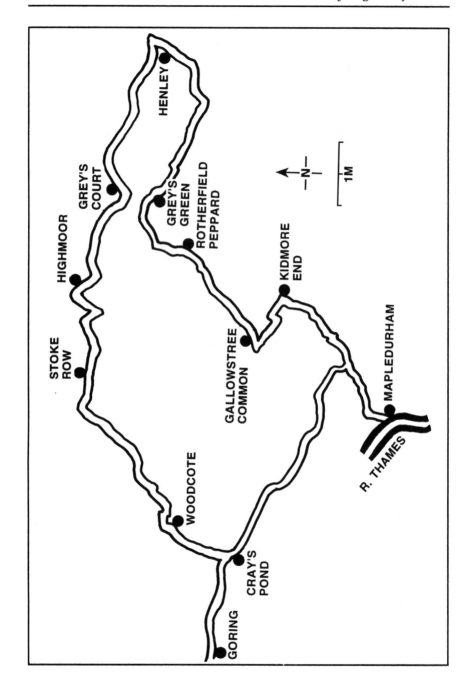

and the village of Rotherfield Peppard to Bolt's Cross where you turn right to Henley. Carry on for about one mile to Greys Green where you turn right at the junction, pass through Rotherfield Greys and follow the road into Henley Town Centre (about two miles).

Mapledurham House

One of the largest Elizabethan houses in Oxfordshire, Mapledurham House dates back to about 1588. Built by the Blount family it has a patterned red brick exterior with stone dressings. The house is said to have been the prototype for Kenneth Grahame's Toad Hall in "Wind in the Willows" (Grahame lived in nearby Pangbourne, found across the river in Berkshire). Another literary connection with Mapledurham was Alexander Pope who frequently visited the beautiful sisters of Martha and Theresa Blount between 1707 and 1715 (for more of Pope's peregrinations around Oxfordshire see under Stanton Harcourt route 5). The house contains a fine collection of 16th and 17th century paintings, original Tudor woodwork and splendid examples of antique furniture. Opening times are limited, telephone 0734 723350 for details.

Mapledurham Watermill

This is the last working watermill on the Thames and it dates back to the 15th century. Wheat is still ground here using the original millstones. The obligatory gift shop sells 100% whole-wheat flour to visitors. Open most Sundays. Enquiries 0734 723350.

One final "literary" reference before leaving Mapledurham – it was used as the setting in the film of "The Eagle has Landed".

Henley-on-Thames

Set just on the Oxfordshire/Berkshire border, Henley is most famous for its Royal Regatta. The Regatta has been held here in the first week of July since 1839. Races are held on the straight mile of river downstream from the bridge. Despite its upper-crust image the town of Henley is pleasant and worth a visit, particularly in summer when the river attracts substantial numbers of visitors. If you feel like a break from pedalling you can take a launch on the river and see the riverside houses of the rich and famous.

Beginning the return journey, leave Henley by turning left opposite the Tourist Information Centre on Market Place into Gravel Hill. Follow the road for about two miles through the town and into open country until you reach Greys Court on your right.

Greys Court

Owned by the National Trust this is a Jacobean Manor set amongst 14th century ruins. The last surviving donkey wheel for drawing water from a 200ft well stands in the old well house. The wheel dates back to Tudor times and donkey power was used until 1914. The gardens of Grey's Court have been developed over many generations and are outstanding. They include a nut avenue, a wisteria walk and the Archbishop's Maze. If you can find your way out you can buy tea in the Cromwellian stables. For opening times telephone 0491 628529.

Just after Grey's Court look out for the single track road on your right and the sign of the Oxfordshire Cycleway. Turn right into the seemingly endless ascent (nearly two miles in fact) through woodland to the end of the road where you turn right still following the Oxfordshire cycleway signs into the B481. Go through the village of Highmoor Cross until you see the left-hand sign to Stoke Row and the Maharaja's Well just after St Paul's Church on your left. Follow the road, for the most part ascending, to Stoke Row where you follow the road through the centre of the village and you will see the Maharaja's Well on your right; see route 8 for information.

Continue through Stoke Row and turn left at the sign post to Checkendon and Woodcote. After about two miles you will come to the give way sign at the busy A4074 road. Dog leg right then left still following the Oxfordshire cycleway signs. Go through the village of Woodcote and turn left by the war memorial at the crossroads into the B471. The sign indicates that Goring is three and a quarter miles away. Follow the road to the crossroads at Cray's Pond where you turn right joining the B4526 road which you climbed up earlier. Enjoy the glide down to the bottom where you turn left to the station.

Routes 11 – 14

The Cotswolds

This famous range of common upland stretches from east of the River Severn to the West of Oxfordshire. With its rolling patchwork fields and farmland, gentle valleys, thatched cottages and golden stone villages, the Cotswolds region has gained a reputation for archetypal English beauty. The Oolite limestone of the area gives the distinctive stone of the dry stone walls and villages. Although usually thought of as yellow, the stone takes on many hues from grey to deep gold honey in colour and varies from village to village.

The Cotswolds have been inhabited for over 9,000 years as the long barrows, hill forts and ancient trackways of the area testify. The exact derivation of the word Cotswolds is uncertain. "Wold" denotes common upland and "Cot" may derive from the old English for "sheep enclosure". Either way, the region is inextricably linked with the sheep farming that brought considerable wealth to the area. The local breed of Cotswold sheep produced an exceptionally fine fleece and the rivers in the valleys provided water power for the mills. Cotswold wool dominated the woollen trade from the 14th century and at one point the area had over 500,000 sheep. Wealthy wool merchants endowed the area with fine houses and churches giving it the quiet opulent feel that it still has today. The trade flourished for several centuries but when it slumped the Cotswolds experienced appalling poverty. Ironically this poverty has led to the Cotswolds becoming a present day tourist area – lack of development in the towns and villages in the 18th and 19th century means that many of them are still preserved almost as they were although today the area is more likely to be protected by preservation orders than lack of wealth. An outstanding example of preservation is the village of Great Tew (see Route 14).

Today they attract increasing streams of visitors, and towns like Burford, the self-proclaimed "Gateway to the Cotswolds", manage to cater to the antiques and Olde Tea Shoppe market whilst retaining an attractive individuality. Many of the villages have become second homes for city dwellers and commuters often form a substantial number amongst the old rural communities. Despite the inexorable change, the landscape has retained its own character and nowhere do you feel this more than whilst cycling through the hillsides and valleys of this beautiful region.

Route 11:
Charlbury – Leafield – Charlbury

Distance: 10 miles.

You can extend the route by continuing to Burford and linking with Route 13. You can also extend it by continuing from Finstock Station to Stonesfield and Wooton and returning from here to Charlbury, linking with Route 12.

Map: Ordnance Survey 164.

Rail Access: The journey starts and finishes at Charlbury Station.

Cycle Shops: None on route.

Tourist Information: None on route.

Special Interest: Wychwood Forest, Charlbury Museum.

Refreshments: Shops and pubs in Charlbury.

General Information

This circular tour traces the road around the ancient woodland of Wychwood Forest (see below) and Cornbury Deer Park. Wychwood Forest is a popular walking area and Oxfordshire County Council provide a useful walking guide. As well as ancient trees, the ride has as a backdrop the rolling Cotswold hills with their patchwork of colour. This route is particularly attractive in the autumn because of the colours of the Forest. As you would expect, this is a fairly hilly route but the hills are not very strenuous and the balance of rises and falls is fairly even. **CAUTION:** beware of low-flying pheasants in the forest!

Route

On leaving Charlbury Station turn left into the B4437 where you immediately start a gentle rise with the Cotswold Hills on your right and Wychwood Forest on your left. After a mile of continuous rising turn left at the sign that says Leafield three miles. You now enter the road through the Forest.

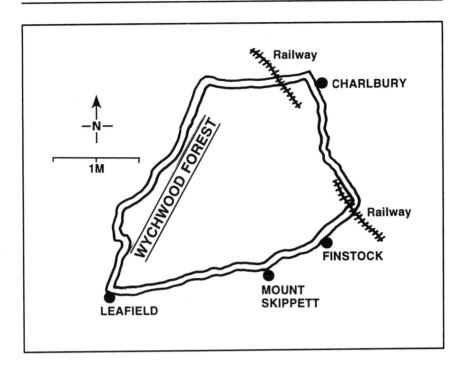

Wychwood Forest

There is evidence of settlement in Wychwood Forest dating back as early as 3,000 BC. In the Middle Ages it was a royal hunting ground used by Edward the Confessor who was born in Islip (see Route 4). It was one of the largest of its kind with many thousands of acres extending as far west as Burford, north to Enstone, east to Blocken and south to Stanton Harcourt. Today only about 2% of the original forest remains.

In the 19th century much of the forest area was turned over to agriculture causing many local villagers to lose their livelihood of grazing animals, and nut and branch gathering. The remaining one and a half thousand acres passed to the owner of Cornbury Park. In 1989 the Ramblers Association earned right of way through the forest and it is now a National Nature Reserve containing 360 species of flowering plants and ferns. The woodland is comprised mainly of oak, beech, maple and ash.

For the most part the forest along this road is fenced in. Pass the entrance to Cornbury Park on your left and the Rangers' house on your right. The road winds and undulates before going into a steep descent. You will see the spire of Leafield Church on the hills ahead before you start climbing steeply up to the junction at Leafield and the parish church of St Michael and All the Angels.

Leafield

Leafield lies on one of the most exposed areas of the Cotswold upland. Its two distinctive features – the church spire and radio masts at the west of the village – can be seen for miles around. In the mid 19th century the glove making industry flourished here (as it did in Charlbury, Burford and Woodstock).

At the junction at Leafield, turn left following the sign to Finstock and Charlbury. Follow the road through ploughed fields and woodland for about three miles towards the cross road at Mount Skippet. Turn left here into the B4022 following the sign to Charlbury. Past the village of Finstock cross over the bridge at Finstock Railway and the road veers round to the left. After about one mile you come to a junction just outside Charlbury. There are two routes through Charlbury. Follow the signs to the town centre which will bring you through golden stone cotswold houses into this small, attractive town.

Charlbury

This small town in the Evenlode Valley has a lovely 13th century church (St Mary's) with a Jacobean oak staircase. The Charlbury Museum on Market Street includes displays of local crafts and industries including hand loom weaving.

At the junction of Sheep Street and Market Street turn left, following the one way sign for about 200 yards where you will see the sign to the station. Enjoy the long swoop down.

Route 12:
Charlbury – Wooton – Rousham – The Bartons – Enstone – Charlbury

Distance: 23 miles.

Few opportunities for cutting this route short

The route can be lengthened by turning right after Rousham and going through the Heyfords, Somerton and the Tews (links with Route 17).

Map: Ordnance Survey Landranger 164.

Rail Access: The journey starts and finishes at Charlbury Station.

Tourist Information: None on route.

Cycle Shops: None on route but Woodstock Bike Shed, 1 Shipton Road, Woodstock is the nearest.

Special Interest: Charlbury, Rousham Park.

Refreshments: Not a well-endowed route The Bull and Bell at Charlbury, Hopcroft's Holt Hotel after Rousham, and a few pubs along the way.

General Description

This route begins in Charlbury on the eastern edge of the Cotswolds and moves further east towards the Cherwell District (named after the River Cherwell) in mid-Oxfordshire. Although less hilly than the more western section of the Cotswolds, this ride contains a fair number of rises and descents. It passes through ancient woodland east of Charlbury, past the far end of Blenheim Palace Estate and through the undulating open farmland of central Oxfordshire.

Route

From Charlbury station turn right into a short, sharp ascent towards the town. You could pay a quick visit to this attractive little town. For details of Charlbury, see ride 2. From Charlbury, go through the town to the junction of the B4022 and the B4437. Veer left into the B4437 and follow the signs to Woodstock (eight miles).

Follow the road through the houses. The road begins to dip and rise through woodland and open fields for about three miles to the impressive Ditchley Gate of the Blenheim Estate. There is no entry here but you can see the Victory Column through the gate on your right.

Ditchley Gate

Anyone who has seen Blenheim Palace (see Route 3) from the usual entrance routes might be forgiven for thinking that this splendid wrought iron edifice is the tradesman's entrance. In fact Ditchley Gate is really the Grand Main Entrance – a two mile drive to the Palace. Unfortunately it is pointing in the wrong direction away from London and for practical purposes has been relegated to the more humble position of back-yard.

From here the road bends to the left towards the A44. Dog leg right then left at the junction by the Duke of Marlborough Pub and follow the sign to Wooton, one mile. Cross the bridge over the River Glyme and begin what feels like a vertical ascent through this attractive stone village. At the top pause to catch your breath, visit the church of St Mary the Virgin and admire the village which has several times been the winner of Oxfordshire's best kept village award.

Carry on to the end of the village and turn right into the B4027 at the sign to Bletchingdon. After about 500 yards turn left at the sign to Rousham three and a half miles. Follow the narrow road up a steep incline and across a plateau of open land, until the road veers right and you come to the busy A4260. Dog leg left then right joining the narrow road to Rousham. After about one mile you will see the sign indicating that Rousham Park is on your right.

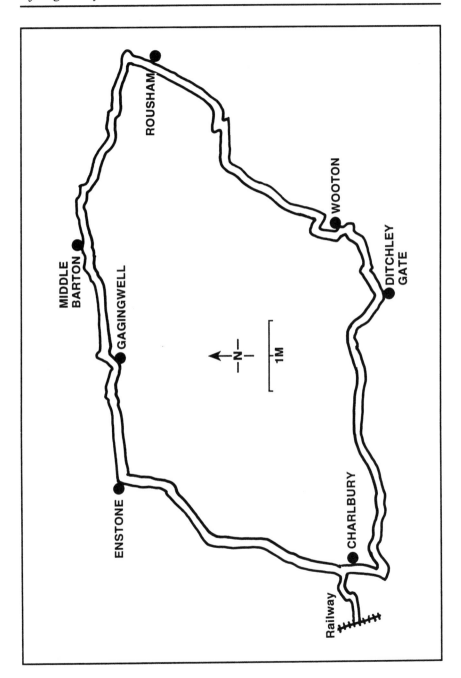

Rousham Park

Overlooking the River Cherwell, Rousham Park House was built in 1635 by Sir Robert Dormer and is still in the same family. The gardens, landscaped by William Kent, have remained almost unchanged and feature terraces, fountains, statues, temples and glades as well as a fake three arched ruin known as "The Eyecatcher". There is also a 17th century pigeon house and a herd of rare Longhorn cattle. The Park has actively resisted commercialisation – there is no tea shop but there are 30 acres in which you're welcome to eat picnic. The garden is open daily.

For details of house opening times, telephone 0869 47110.

After Rousham continue on the route to the junction and turn left at the sign to Enstone six miles and the Bartons (B4030). A rise of about half a mile brings you back to the A4260 where you dog leg right and left past Holcroft's Holt Hotel following the B4030 to the various Bartons – Barton Gate, Middle Barton and Westcott Barton. About one mile from Westcott Barton the road veers left at the hamlet of Gagingwell then right past the Enstone Airfield (famous locally for its gliding club). On your left is a disused quarry and you take the next turning left into the B4022 at the sign to Enstone and Charlbury. A steep climb of about half a mile brings you back to the A44. dog leg right and left to Charlbury rejoining the B4022. After a mile the road veers to the left and you finally come to a nice long descent into the town centre of Charlbury.

Route 13:
Charlbury – Swinbrook – Burford – Witney – Charlbury

Distance: 28¹/₂ miles.

You can shorten the journey by returning to Charlbury via Minster Lovell, Leafield and Finstock. Various opportunities for lengthening eg. via Woodstock from Finstock and joining with Route 12.

Maps: Ordnance Survey Landranger 164 and 163.

Rail Access: The journey starts and finishes at Charlbury Station.

Tourist Information: Burford, The Old Brewery, Sheep Street, Witney, 51a Market Square.

Cycle Shops: Dentons, 1 High Street Witney, Norridge; 134 Brize Norton Road, Minster Lovell.

Special Interest: Swinbrook Church, Burford Museum, the Cotswold Wildlife Park, Minster Lovell Hall, Cogges Farm.

Refreshments: Plenty of tea shops and pubs in Burford and in Witney, cafeteria at Cogges Farm, Pubs in Charlbury.

General Description

This is arguably one of the most attractive parts of Oxfordshire, set as it is against the backdrop of rolling Cotswold hills and characterized by patchwork fields, rich red earth and the occasional forested area. Steeped in a long history of sheep farming, the area is still used as grazing land today and evidence of its connection with the wool trade can be seen in the blanket mills at Witney. For the most part, however, this route is purely scenic and greatly enhanced by the lovely village of Swinbrook lying on the River Windrush from where the route follows the meandering path of the river to Burford, the Gateway to the Cotswolds. Inevitably, where the scenery is at its best there are hills so be prepared for a few lengthy climbs – the views will be well worth it.

Route

On leaving Charlbury station, turn left into the B4437 from where you soon catch sight of Wychwood forest to your left (see Route 11) and hills to your right. After about one mile of gentle rising you will see the sign to Burford seven miles straight ahead. Follow the road for about five miles as it contours around the hills and dips and rises. Look out for the crossroads and the sign to Swinbrook where you turn left, now joining part of the Oxfordshire Cycleway. Enjoy a long descent to the village of Swinbrook.

Swinbrook

Set in the Windrush Valley Swinbrook seems set back in time. Its large houses, cottages, village green and babbling brook make the village seem like a monument to preservation. The Swinbrook estate was in the hands of the Fettiplace family until 1806 but want of a male heir meant that it passed out of the family.

The 13th century parish church of St Mary's contains a remarkable Fettiplace memorial depicting two trios of reclining members of the family. Other points of interest at St Mary's are the graves of the author Nancy Mitford and of her sister Unity whose curious affection for Hitler led to her suicide. Their father, Lord Redesdale, built South Lawn House in 1926.

From Swinbrook carry on through the village, over the bridge crossing the Windrush with the Swan Inn on your right. At the next crossroads turn right following the sign to Burford two and a quarter miles and still on the Oxfordshire cycle way where it intersects the Windrush Valley Route (see under Route 20). Follow the road along the route of the river for just over a mile to the give way sign where you turn right to Burford one and a quarter miles and follow this road until it takes you through the quiet back street entrance to Burford. At the end of the road, at the corner of Andrews Hotel and Walkers Garden Statuary shop you are in the long descending road of Burford's main street.

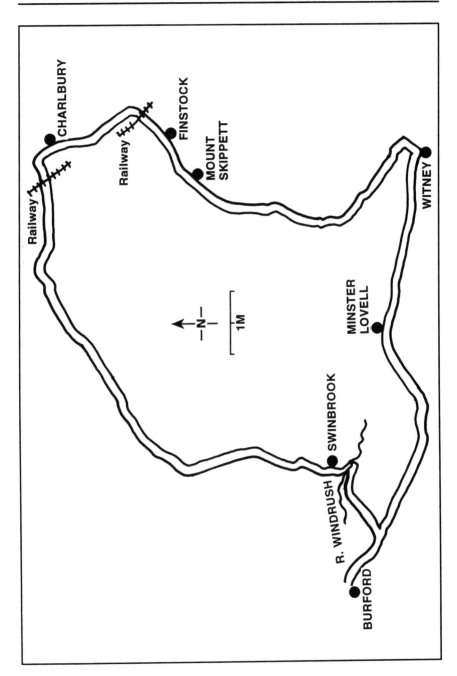

Burford

Set close to the Gloucestershire border, Burford had been a major Cotswold crossroad for centuries. Known as the "Gateway to the Cotswolds", the town itself consists of a long main street sweeping down to the River Windrush. The name "Bur ford" means defended settlement by a ford. As with many Cotswold towns, Burford has links with the Wool Trade and flourished as a market town for many centuries. Today you are more likely to find antique shops and tea shops but the Tolsey Museum on the High Street (built in an early Tudor Court House) recreates Burford's social and industrial past.

Cotswold Wildlife Park

While in Burford you can visit the nearby Cotswold Wildlife Park which is on the A361, two miles south of its junction with the A40. It is not a testimony to Cotswold animal life but an open air zoo with animals from all over the world. There is something rather incongruous about the sight of rhinos and zebras grazing around a neo-Gothic Cotswold manor house but it takes all kinds.

Leave Burford via the road you came on (you will have to push your bicycle a little way because it is a one way street). Follow the road back to the junction and carry straight on following the signs to Witney (six miles). A short, sharp rise brings you on to the A40. Turn left and proceed with care. The beautiful views down to the valley and on your right almost make up for the juggernauts on this part on the route.

After nearly a mile and a half you reach a roundabout near the Windmill Restaurant. Veer left here, leaving the A road for the B4047, following the signs to Minster Lovell (there's a picnic site 150 yards on) and Minster Lovell Hall and the Cogges Museum.

Minster Lovell Hall

Turn off left at the signpost and cross over the Windrush to visit Minster Lovell Hall. This ruined manor house on the banks of the Windrush dates back to the 15th century. Legend goes that during the War of the Roses the owner, Francis Lovell, supported the Yorkists. After defeat he is supposed to have taken refuge in the Hall, hiding in a secret room where he died of starvation. In the early 18th century workmen discovered a skeleton in a secret chamber. The skeleton crumbled to dust on being exposed to air. John Buchan recounts this legend in the novel "The Blanket of the Dark" (see also Route 4 on Buchan).

A Cotswold cottage, Minster Lovell

Follow the B4047 for about two miles past Minster Lovell and into increasingly urban and industrialised surroundings. You can bypass the sprawl and Witney by turning left at the sign for Crawley. Otherwise carry on for about another mile to Witney's attractive town centre. Whilst at Witney you may want to pay a visit to Cogges Farm Museum.

Witney

Witney is famous for its blankets and this industry dates back to the 13th century. The town's position by the River Windrush made it ideal for powering water wheels that could drive looms. Blanket Hall in the High Street was built in 1721 and served as a place for blankets to be weighed and measured – an early form of quality control. Today there are three mills in operation in Witney. The Blanket firm of Charles Early Ltd is one of the oldest trading companies in Britain.

Cogges Farm Museum

This is an Edwardian era farm which recreates rural life at the turn of the century. There are demonstrations of everything from lambing to lace making. There is a picnic area and cafeteria.

Leave Witney by the B4022, and veer left off it following the road to Crawley. At Crawley carry straight on at the crossroads, following the sign to Minster Lovell and Leafield. After rising veer right at the sign to Charlbury. After about one mile veer left again onto the B4022, following the sign to Charlbury four a half miles.

Follow the road, passing a few small hamlets, to Mount Skippett and past Wychwood forest on your left. By-pass Finstock and carry on as the road descends to Finstock Railway, veers left and rises again towards Charlbury. At the junction turn left and carry on to the town centre and turn left into the main road opposite the Pub. Carry on to the sign left towards Charlbury Station and enjoy the long sweep down.

Route 14:
Kingham – Churchill – Chipping Norton – The Rollright Stones – Great Tew – Enstone – Churchill – Kingham

Distance: 30 miles.

There are limited opportunities for cutting this route short unless you cut out points of interest like the Rollright Stones and Great Tew.

Various ways of lengthening the route by proceeding further north from the Rollrights to Hook Norton and Banbury (links with Route 15) or further east from Great Tew to Duns Tew, Somerton, The Heyfords and Enstone (links with Route 17).

Maps: This route straddles several – Ordnance Survey Landranger 163, 164, 151.

Rail Access: The journey starts and finishes at Kingham Station.

Tourist Information: Chipping Norton, Guild Hall.

Cycle Shops: Reeve Cycles, Banbury Road, Chipping Norton.

Special Interest: The Rollright Stones, Great Tew.

Refreshments: Tea shops and restaurants at Chipping Norton and Wyatt's Farm Shop and Tea Rooms after the Rollright Stones. The Falkland Arms at Great Tew.

General Description

This route takes in more of the northern section of the Oxfordshire Cotswolds. There are some hills which might slow you down. For the most part it is far removed from urban civilisation with Chipping Norton (see below) being the only town. The route also takes in the prehistoric Rollright stones and the village of Great Tew which must be a strong contender for the nation's most picturesque village.

Route

On leaving Kingham Station turn left into the B4450, crossing over the Railway Bridge. Carry on for about one third of a mile to where the road veers right and follow the sign that tells you Churchill is two miles away and Chipping Norton four. Follow the road as it winds and dips and soars to the village of Churchill.

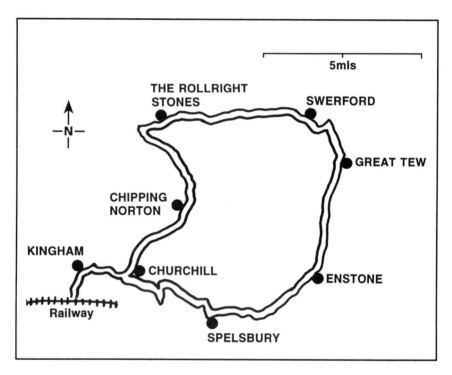

At Churchill follow the signs to Chipping Norton (still on the B4450). There is now a straightforward run of about three miles to Chipping Norton. As you approach the town look out for the Mill in the valley to your left.

Follow the road, crossing over the mini-roundabout straight into the town centre.

Churchill

This iattractive village of golden Cotswold Stone is not named after its eminent namesakes at Blenheim Palace twelve miles away (see Route 3). The village is dominated by the towering tower of All Saints Church in the centre. The church is a relatively modern construction and was only consecrated in 1827 thanks to the patronage of local squire John Langston. The tower is of special interest – it is a replica of Magdalen College tower in Oxford but is only two thirds the size. Famous sons of Churchill include Warren Hastings, Governor General of Bengal and William Smith, father of British geology.

Bliss's Mill

Set comfortably in the small valley just outside Chipping Norton, Bliss's Mill is a lingering link with the industrial past. It was built in 1746 and manufactured horse cloth before changing to serge and tweed in the 19th century. The Mill was still producing tweed until 1980 and has now been converted into flats whilst retaining its distinctive central chimney.

Chipping Norton

The name means "northern market town" but to locals it's always called "Chippy". Situated in the highest part of Oxfordshire it is a lively Cotswold Market Town once famous for its wool trade and now has its own theatre, tourist information centre and sports centre. Prosperous and pretty and not as "touristy" as Burford it has attractive 17th century almshouses, a museum and a good number of pubs and restaurants. The central Market Square was once the venue for an important annual sheep fair.

Leave Chipping Norton by continuing to the mini roundabout at the end of the main street and turn left here into the B4026, following the signs to Great Rollright three miles and the Rollright Stones. Prepare for a steep descent then rise to the village of Over Norton. Follow the road round to the right and look out for the left turn in the centre of the village and the sign to Little Rollright and the Rollright Stones.

After more rising there is a sharp descent and a glorious view of patchwork fields. Follow the signs to Little Rollright and the Stones. Carry on for about two miles of long, long ascent to the stop sign and stunning views. Catch your breath and turn right following the signs for the Stones. The Stones are about half a mile further on and are secluded behind hedges so are not immediately obvious.

The Rollright Stones

There are three separate sites to the Rollright Stones. On the right (on this route) and the largest is "The King's Men" stone circle. Rumour has it that it is impossible to count the stones twice and come up with the same number but 77 seems to have become the accepted total by common consensus.

The Rollright Stones

Across the road (and across the border into Warwickshire) is the King Stone – a single eight foot pillar surrounded by railings which stands in splendid but bent isolation. A little further down the road on the right a trackway takes you to the "Whispering Knights" comprising four upright stones and thought to be a neolithic barrow.

These Bronze Age stones date back to about 1500 BC. They are not quite in the same league as Stonehenge but still exert an attraction over 20th century pagans. The obligatory legend tells of how a king and his army came to conquer England and in this spot they met a witch. The witch told the King:

> *"Seven long strides thou shalt take*
> *And if Long Compton thou can see*
> *King of England thou shalt be"*

On failing to see Long Compton (about one mile north) the king and his men were turned into stone. The Whispering Knights are separate because they are supposed to have been plotting against the king at the time of petrifaction. It is said that all the stone figures get the night off occasionally to go down to Little Rollright to drink water. On Midsummer's day the sun is supposed to rise directly behind the King Stone.

When you've finished carry on (note the sign for Wyatt's tea shop) to the give way sign about half a mile away at the junction of the A3400. You are now in the no-person's land of the Warwickshire and Oxfordshire border. Dog leg right then immediately left following the signs to Great Rollright (one and a half miles) and Hook Norton. On your left you will find Wyatt's Farm Shop. Stop for a cup of tea and admire the views.

About 200 yards from Wyatts turn right following the sign to Great Rollright half a mile and the Oxfordshire Cycleway. Carry on to and through Great Rollright now following the sign to Swerford three and a half miles away. After about quarter of a mile the road veers to the left but carry straight on down the single track road still following the signs to Swerford. Continue to the steep descent which takes you down to this pretty stone village followed by an even steeper ascent to the give way sign at the A361. Turn left here and then first right at the sign to Enstone five miles and The Tews into the B4022 and descend and rise for a mile until you see the sign to the left to St Michael's Church and Great Tew.

Great Tew

By far the prettiest village in the county, Great Tew has been called "the place where time stood still". The rich golden stone and thatched cottages, the village green and The Falkland Arms Pub all contribute to the picture postcard beauty of the village. Great Tew is an estate village with a record 69 listed buildings.

When you've finished return to the B4022 and rise and fall for about three miles to the road junction. Dog leg right then left following the signs to Enstone and still following the B4022. After just over half a mile ascend to the give way sign at the junction of the A44 and dog leg over right then left following the signs to Charlbury and Spelsbury on the

B4022. After a mile you will see the sign to Spelsbury one and a quarter miles on your right. At Spelsbury proceed to the junction and follow the sign to Chadlington one and a half miles. At Chadlington look out for the sign at the crossroads by the Citroen garage where you turn right following the sign to Churchill three and a half miles. After about quarter of a mile follow the sign left to Churchill.

There now follows a long ascent to the A361 where you dog leg left and right and carry on to Churchill until you enter the village via a steep hill which will bring you back opposite the Church. From here follow the previous route back to Kingham.

Routes 15 – 17

The Cherwell District

Found in north eastern Oxfordshire and named after the River Cherwell, the Cherwell District comprises three distinct types of landscape. To the north around Banbury are red, low-lying hills coloured by underlying ironstone which is apparent in the golden coloured stone of the villages in this area. Further South around Bicester (pronounced Bister) are low limestone hills – an eastern extension of the oolite limestone of the Cotswolds. Southwards again is an area of low clay land stretching to the Ray Valley and to the fenny area of Otmoor.

The Cherwell itself rises in Northamptonshire and is a narrow shallow river which stretches southwards to Oxford and has been made unduly famous as the leafy punting ground for Oxford students. Following the line of the Cherwell is the Oxford Canal which runs parallel to it (as can be seen in Route 17). Oxford Canal, completed in 1790 runs from the junction with the Grand Union at Napton to the heart of the City of Oxford and was an important route for transporting coal to the district until it was superseded by the railway (running along the same route) in the 1840s.

Among the Cherwell District's more famous inhabitants was Flora Thompson born in 1876 at Juniper Hill, a hamlet of Cottisford (see route 17). Author of "Lark Rise to Candleford", she left a portrait of country life and tradition in the area. A second book "Still Glides the Stream" was published in 1948. Crafts of the area which Thompson recalls are quarrying, weaving and lace making. The crafts of the Cherwell District are now largely things of the past but "Lark Rise to Candleford" vividly captures a lost era in the Cherwell District.

Route 15:
Banbury – Broughton – Swalcliffe – Sibford Ferris – Hook Norton – Bloxham – Banbury

Distance: 19 miles. You can cut the journey short by turning left at Swalcliffe to Wiggington Heath and rejoining the route at Milcombe. You can lengthen the route by continuing from Hook Norton to Deddington and returning via Aynho and Adderbury. The Route links with Route 16 at Broughton.

Map: Ordnance Survey Landranger 151.

Rail Access: The journey starts and finishes at Banbury Station.

Tourist Information: Banbury, Banbury Museum, Horsefair.

Cycle Shops: Banbury Cycles Ltd., 54 Bridge Street. Banbury. Garden Machinery 2 Bridge Street. Trinder Bros. ltd, 56/59 Broad Street, Banbury.

Special Interest: Banbury Cross and Museum, Broughton Castle and Park, Swalcliffe Barn, Bloxham village museum.

Refreshments: tea shops, restaurants and pubs in Banbury, tea room at Broughton Castle, pubs in Hook Norton.

General Description

This route takes in some of the attractive villages and farmland just south of Oxford's most northern town, Banbury. The first part of the journey to Hook Norton contains a number of hills but from Hook Norton back to Banbury is fairly easy cycling. The landscape is mainly of hills and fields and this area tends to be greener than the patchwork Cotswold hills further south. Despite the encroachment of the 20th century and modern housing developments there are still a fair number of thatched cottages in this area and places where the yellow stone from the Cotswolds has turned almost orange with age. Sibford Ferris and Hook Norton are the most attractive examples of villages on the route whilst the castle at Broughton offers a glimpse of a less humble dwelling.

Route

On leaving Banbury Station turn left and go to the traffic lights at the cross roads. Carry straight over the cross road towards the town centre and at the mini-roundabout push your bike through the pedestrian centre following the signs to the Tourist Information centre and the Banbury Cross. The tourist information centre is just beyond the shops on the left opposite the Banbury Cross in Horsefair and the Banbury museum is here too.

Banbury

Famous for the nursery rhyme "Ride a Cock Horse" (see below) and for its spicy cakes, Banbury is situated north of the Cherwell District of Oxfordshire and is the county's second largest town. The town dates back to Saxon times and still hosts one of the oldest cattle markets in Britain. Today it is a thriving, prosperous town with a large modern shopping centre but you can catch some of the flavour of the past in the Banbury Museum. Housed in the old boardroom of the Poor Law Guardians, the Museum tells the story of "Banburyshire". The Tourist Office is situated here as well over-looking the Banbury Cross of the nursery rhyme.

Banbury Cross

The Cross in Horsefair is not the original – there have been several, and there were three in medieval times. The present one dates back only to 1859 and was built to celebrate the marriage of Queen Victoria's eldest daughter to Prince Frederic of Prussia.

The Nursery Rhyme

This is centuries old and survived in oral tradition until the 18th century when it first appeared in print. The reference to the cock horse probably refers to the medieval practice of two people riding the same horse – the knight in front and his lady behind. Today the fast intercity service between London and Birmingham has rendered the practice somewhat obsolete but cyclists are recommended to ring their bells when negotiating the busy roundabout at the Cross anyway.

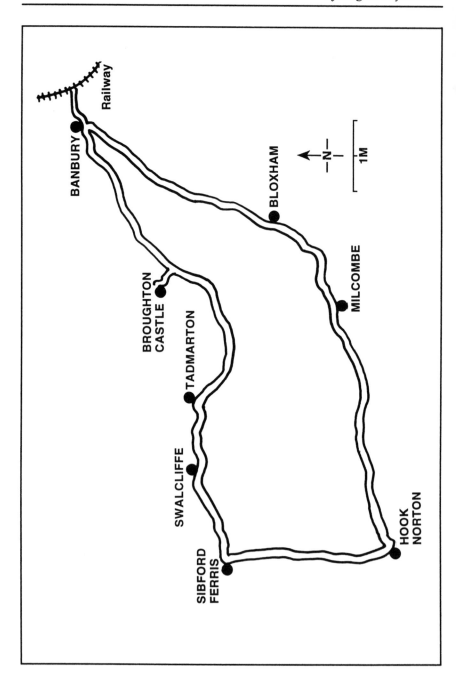

Go straight over the roundabout onto Broughton Road (the B4035) and follow the route to Broughton through the residential area leading to a second roundabout where you go straight on. From here the residential area is replaced by open countryside and you carry on for about three miles from Banbury where you will see the sign to Broughton Castle on your right next to the Saye and Sele Arms pub. Turn right and follow the narrow road down to the entrance to Broughton Park.

Broughton Castle and Park

Surrounded by a moat, Broughton Castle is a splendid example of a 14th century castle. Built in 1300 by the Fiennes family of the Lords Saye and Sele, the Castle has remained their ancestral seat for over 600 years (famous family members include Celia Fiennes, the 17th century traveller and Sir Ranulph the 20th century explorer). Features of the castle include a Medieval Great Hall, vaulted passages, arms and armour from the Civil War and the obligatory tea room and shop. Opening times are limited, telephone 0295 262624 or check with Banbury Tourist information.

On leaving Broughton Castle return back to the B4035, turn right and follow the signs to Tadmarton. Pass through Lower Tadmarton and through the long linear village of Tadmarton. From here follow the signs to Swalcliffe.

NOTE: you can also do a detour left from Lower Tadmorton to the Wiggington Water Fowl Trust. This is a rescue centre for a wide variety of domesticated animals and birds and – if you feel like it – there's an adventure playground too. After more rises and falls you arrive at the village of Swalcliffe. Look out on your right, just past the church, for Swalcliffe Barn.

Swalcliffe Barn

Swalcliffe means "shallow cliff where swallows nested". The manor of Swalcliffe belonged to William of Wykeham who built a large tithe barn here in the early 15th century. The barn comprises 10 bays and is one of the most substantial in England. Much of the medieval timber roof is still intact and visitors can see collections of agricultural trade vehicles. For details of opening times telephone 0295 788278.

On leaving Swalcliffe proceed up the hill for just under half a mile and look out for the sign to the left to Sibford Ferris. Turn left and go to Sibford Ferris.

Sibford Ferris

The twin villages of Sibford Gower and Sibford Ferris face each other across the steep valley of the River Stour. Sibford Ferris houses Sibford School – one of only nine Quaker Schools in England.

Enjoy the descent through the centre of this lovely village and follow the road round to the left before another descent and a gentler ascent to the give way sign where you carry straight on following the signs to Hook Norton.

Hook Norton

Hook Norton is best known for its local ale "Old Hookey" which has been brewed here since 1849. This real Ale is brewed by traditional methods in the red brick Victorian brewery at the west end of the village in the predictably named "Brewery Lane". The parish church of St Peter dates back to Norman times and the font inside has lovely carvings of Adam and Eve and signs of the Zodiac. Also of interest is the Hook Norton Pottery – a working pottery with displays and items for sale.

At the stop sign at the end of the road where you came into Hook Norton turn left and soon you will see the sign to Banbury 8 miles. Follow the road out of the village and pay a visit to Hook Norton Pottery on your right. From here the route rises and falls more gently through hillsides and green pasture. After about four miles pass through the unremarkable village of Milcombe to the give way sign. Turn left here following the sign to Banbury into the A361 and continue for about half a mile to Bloxham.

Bloxham

An extensive village, Bloxham is especially noted for the dominating spire of the 14th century church of St Mary's. Also of interest is the Bloxham Village Museum housed in the Old Court House. The collection reflects past rural life in the village.

From Bloxham you can continue on the A361 which will bring you directly to the centre of Banbury or turn left to Broughton at the end of the village rejoining the route you took out of Banbury.

Banbury Cross

Route 16:
Banbury – Broughton – Hornton – Cropedy – Banbury

Distance: $22^1/_2$ miles.

Several opportunities to cut the route short – omit the section from Wroxton to Hornton and go directly to Horley. From Williamscot follow the A361 directly to Banbury. From Horley turn right to Banbury along B4100. You can lengthen the journey by linking up with route 15 at Broughton.

Maps: Ordnance Survey Landranger 151.

Rail Access: The journey starts and finishes at Banbury Station.

Tourist Information: Banbury, Banbury Museum, Horsefair.

Cycle Shops: Banbury Cycles Ltd, 54 Bridge Street, Banbury; Banbury Garden Machinery, 2 Bridge Street, Banbury; Trinder Bros Ltd, 56 – 59 Broad Street, Banbury.

Special Interest: Banbury Museum, Broughton Castle.

Refreshments: Banbury, tea rooms Broughton, Cropedy Coal wharf serves tea in season.

General Description

This round tour takes in the area mainly to the north of Banbury. For the most part the landscape is open farmland and hills of rich red soil which characterises this area. Although generally the terrain is more gentle than the Cotswolds to the south, the Route is distinctly hilly in parts and be prepared for low gears in places. That said, the route is quiet, unspoilt and there are some stunning views.

Route

Leaving Banbury Station turn left and after about 200 yards go across the traffic lights, following the signs to the town centre. Ahead you will see

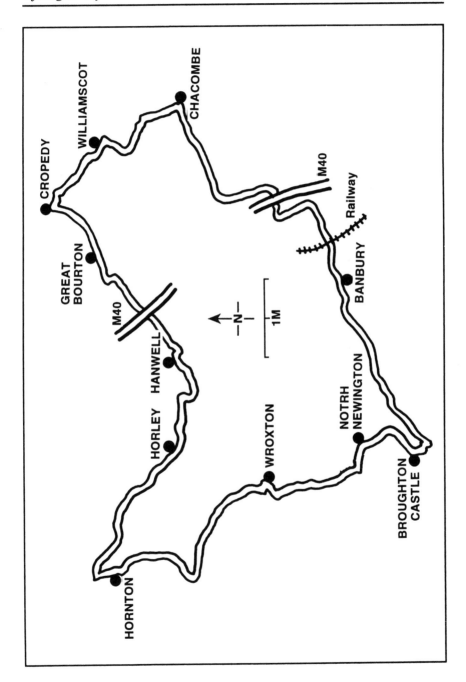

the town hall. At the mini-roundabout by the town hall, walk your bike through the pedestrian precinct following the signs to the famous Cross and the Banbury Museum in Horse Fair. See the previous ride for details of Banbuery.

Go over the road, past the Cross into Broughton Road (the B4035). Ride through this residential area, going straight over the roundabout and follow the road for a further two miles until you see the signs right to Broughton Castle by the Saye and Sele pub. Turn right down the narrow descending lane to the castle grounds entrance. Bicycles are not allowed. See the previous ride for details of Broughton Castle and Park.

When you leave the castle grounds veer left and then right at the fork in the road. After half a mile turn left and follow the sign to North Newington. There is a steep rise and fall through this attractive village of golden stone. At the end of the village take the first turning on the right (not always sign posted) to Wroxton.

The road rises steeply before becoming more gentle for one and a half miles. At the give way sign turn right into the A422 then take the first left turn out of the pleasant but uninspiring village of Wroxton, following the sign post to Hornton three miles. The single track road takes you through several ups and downs to Hornton. Go through the village and be prepared for more rising and falling before a roller coaster down to the village of Hornton and an equally steep ascent up out of it. Catch your breath at the top and enjoy the feeling of being on top of the world before turning right, following the signs to Horley. You have now reached a plateau and enjoy the magnificent views of rolling hillside before another sheer descent into Horley.

At the crossroads turn left at the sign to Banbury. Ride for about one mile until the junction with the B4100 at the top of a steep hill. Dog leg right then left at the sign to Hanwell. Ride through this pretty thatched village then cross over the M40. About half a mile from the M40 dog leg left onto the A423 then right, following the signs to Great Bourton and Cropedy. Go through Great Bourton with its golden stone cottages and after about one mile go under the railway bridge to come to the less attractive (but by no means unpleasing) village of Cropedy.

Cropedy

This village by the Oxford Canal and the River Cherwell was the site of the Civil War Battle of Cropedy Bridge which took place in 1644. Most of the fighting was in the low-lying meadows just east of the Bridge. History records that there was no decisive victory here either for the King or the Parliamentarians. Today the village is relatively peaceful and a popular spot for canal boat owners.

From Cropedy take the sign right to Williamscot and Wardington. The road leads you to the Oxford Canal and the Old Coal Wharf. Try the Old Coal Wharf for its tea shop and art gallery if it is open.

From the wharf cross over the canal bridge and follow the road to yet another pretty village, Williamscot. After Williamscot dog leg right into the A361 then left to Chacombe. The single track road takes you briefly across the border into Northamptonshire before you turn right at the junction following the sign to Banbury four miles. The route enters low-lying farmland now. At the end of the road turn left along the busy A361 (the sign says Banbury two and a quarter). Follow the road to the roundabout where you turn right to Banbury with GREAT CARE. Carry on to the second roundabout where you turn left, following the sign to the cattle market. At the next roundabout by the garage turn right into Middleton Road and follow the route back to the station.

Route 17:
Bicester – The Heyfords – Deddington – Bicester

Distance: 30 miles.

Maps: Ordnance Survey Landranger 164 and 151.

Rail Access: The journey starts and finishes at Bicester Station.

Tourist Information: None on route.

Cycle Shops: Broadribbs 83 – 85 Sheep Street, Bicester; The Cyclogical Shop, Garage Courtyard, Hudson Street, Deddington.

Special Interest: Deddington Castle, Aynho Park, Cottisford and Flora Thompson.

Refreshments: shops in Bicester, pubs in villages *en route* and in Deddington.

General Description

Starting in the historic town of Bicester (see below), this route takes in the flat lying areas of east Oxfordshire close to the borders with Buckinghamshire. It goes northwards towards the multi-coloured foothills of the Cotswolds south of Banbury. Just west of Bicester is the Cherwell District and from Lower Heyford to Somerton the route runs parallel to the valley of the Cherwell River and the Oxfordshire Canal offering beautiful views to the west. There are several attractive villages *en route* built in the mellow golden stone of the area and there is a good sprinkling of thatch cottages. There is some climbing from the Heyfords to Deddington but the scenery makes it well worth it.

Route

From Bicester Town Station turn left towards the Town Centre (about quarter of a mile away if that). About 500 yards from the station you can turn left into the A421 which you follow to the junction with the A4095 which brings you, after a mile into the B4030. Before going down this route you may want to pay a visit to Bicester.

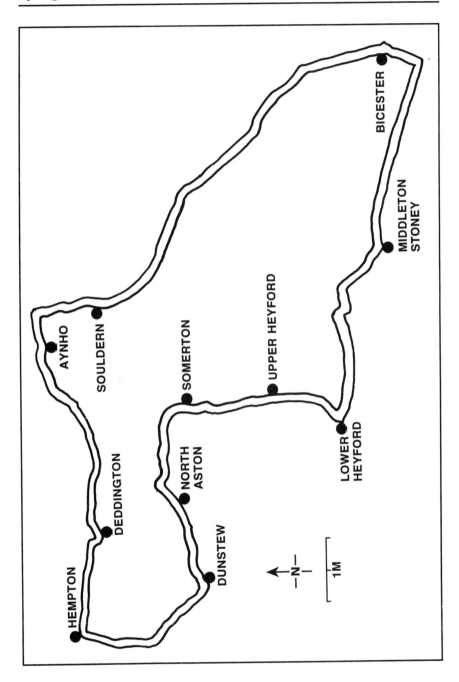

Bicester

Bicester (pronounced 'Bister'), as the name suggests, is a market town with Roman origins. The town has enjoyed mixed fortunes over the centuries. In the 12th century it was a prosperous market town but was severely affected by the Black Death. Fortunes revived in the 16th and 17th century but the town was scourged by smallpox and a series of devastating fires in the early 18th century. Fortunes revived again in the 19th century and today Bicester is an expanding town, absorbing some of the overspill from nearby Oxford.

Follow the B4030 for nearly two miles, across flat open country and across the bridge over the M40 towards Middleton Stoney. At the junction follow the signs to the Heyfords, Bartons and Enstone opposite the Jersey arms. Carry straight on past Middleton Park. After about one mile there is a sign right to RAF Upper Heyford. If you want to see the sprawling mass of the American base turn up here and then veer left to come out at Upper Heyford. For the more scenic route carry on along the B4030 to Lower Heyford where you turn right. The road now rises to Upper Heyford and Somerton with the backdrop of the Cherwell River, the Oxford Canal and the valley on your left.

The Heyfords

The name Heyford probably indicates the presence of a ford used at the hay harvest. Set beside the River Cherwell, both have an archetypal English village feel to them. This is marred somewhat by the vast sprawling presence of Upper Heyford Airfield to the right of the higher village – an eerie presence in this beautiful valley.

At Somerton veer left to North Aston and descend to cross the bridges over the Canal and the Cherwell and rise to the attractive village of North Aston with its village green. From North Aston follow the road to the A4260. Go straight over to Duns Tew (part of the three Tews), and just beyond this pretty village look out for the road which takes you right towards Hempton two and a quarter miles and the Barfords.

This road is relatively flat before rising in to what feels like a very steep climb (definitely low gears time) to the junction of the B4031 and the mellow golden stone village of Hempton. Turn right here following the signs to Deddington and Aynho. On the pavement of the road to Deddington is a cycle path which you can use up to Deddington, one and a half miles away. The road runs through Deddington until the junction at the A4260. Go straight over and still on the B4031 follow the road through the town.

Deddington

A beautiful little town in golden stone, Deddington was a Saxon settlement – originally the Town of Daeda's People. The remnants of Deddington castle mound (on your right as you follow the road past the church and out of the town) is not very noteworthy although it was here that Edward II's favourite, Piers Gaveston, was taken prisoner by the Earl of Warwick. The present architecture in Deddington is a mishmash of 17th and 18th century with the lovely almshouses in Church Street dating back to 1818. The commanding church dates back to the 13th century but also contains 17th century Gothic.

After Deddington follow the road to the small village of Clifton just over a mile away, cross the Cherwell (into Northamptonshire) just after and then go over the canal and railway and M40 for a climb up to the junction at Aynho. Whilst you pause to get your breath here look for the stocks on the small green on your left. These were built in the early 18th century and last used in 1860. They are behind railings now so you can't use them as a resting place so turn right towards Souldern and Bicester Follow the road as it veers to the right then left with Aynho Park on your right.

Aynho Park

The name was originally "Aienho" meaning a spring or grove on a hill. This magnificent 17th century house was remodelled by John Soame and has lovely unspoilt views across the surrounding hillsides. It is now in private ownership but a few rooms are open to the public. Limited opening times, telephone 0869 810636.

Continue past the park to the turn right into the B4100 towards Bicester by-passing the village of Souldern on your right. The route now takes you directly for six miles back to Bicester and is signposted.

Alternately you could follow the route to Cottisford, close to the hamlet of Juniper Hill made famous by Flora Thompson in "Lark Rise to Candleford". To get there continue straight ahead in Aynho into the

B4031 instead of turning into the B4100. Continue along the B4031, past Croughton to the A43 where you turn right then left to Cottisford.

Flora Thompson

Flora Thompson was born at Juniper Hill in 1876 and worked there as the postmistress assistant. Her most famous autobiographical work, "Larkrise to Candleford" was published in 1939 and describes what was even then a disappearing rural way of life. In the work, Thompson draws a sharp distinction between the reserved superiority of the village at Cottisford and the earthy friendliness of the hamlet at Juniper Hill. With its close attention to local detail the book is a remarkable portrait of a by-gone age.

You can return to Bicester by carrying on from Cottisford to the A421 where you turn right and it will bring you back into the town centre of Bicester.

Routes 18 – 19

The Vale of the White Horse

Stretching from south west Oxfordshire towards Didcot, the Vale of the White Horse is one of Oxfordshire's loveliest natural assets. The Vale is named after the prehistoric monument carved into the white chalk of the downs west of Wantage. This area seems to have been almost over-endowed with archaeological gifts from pre-historic times (see especially route 19) and to cycle through it is to have a privileged sense of riding through ancient history. The market town of Wantage is the birth place of Alfred the Great and St George is said to have slayed the Dragon on the nearby downs. In more recent times, the area saw the arrival of Brunel's Great Western Railway at Didcot. Stretching from Bristol to London, the railway was instrumental in opening up the region to commerce and travel in the 19th century. Despite this, the area is not well-endowed with railway stations and route 19 entails a journey over the border into Swindon in Wiltshire.

The Vale is a largely rural area and the Vale and downland Museum Centre at Wantage recreates agricultural life in the area and has an interpretative display of the landscape of the Vale.

The ancient track of the Ridgeway passes over the hills of the Vale making it a popular walkers' spot but the region has strongly resisted the encroachment of tourism and its picturesque villages, characterised by chalk brick and timber, seem also to belong to a long gone past. The downs in the south western part of the Vale form the border with Berkshire and offer exceptional views over the flat northern part of the Vale. The area is strongly identified with Berkshire as in 1974 the old county of Oxfordshire disappeared and the new county incorporated this section of the Vale of White Horse. It was Berkshire's loss and Oxfordshire's gain.

Route 18:
Didcot – Sutton Courtenay – Wantage – Didcot

Distance: 29 miles. Few opportunities to cut short but by turning left at East Hanney onto the A338 through Grove and Wantage you can reduce it by about seven and a half miles. You can lengthen the route by linking with route 19, continuing west from Wantage.

Map: Ordnance Survey Landranger 174.

Rail Access: The journey starts and finishes at Didcot Station.

Tourist Information: There is no official centre on the route but the Vale and Downland Museum, Church Street, Wantage has information on areas of local interest.

Cycle Shops: Dentons, 133 The Broadway, Didcot; Grove Auto Spares, 9 Millbrook Square, Grove; A L Vickers at Drayton is an ironmongery and hardware shop but it also sells cycle spares.

Special Interest: Didcot Railway Centre, George Orwell's and Lord Asquith's grave at Sutton Courtenay, Wantage Vale and Downland Museum Centre.

Refreshments: Shops and pubs in Wantage and a pleasant refreshment bar and picnic area at the Vale and Downland Museum.

General Description

This route takes in some of the low-lying district in the eastern section of the Vale of the White Horse. The fairly straight roads and flat fields give the area an almost Low Country feel in places, especially along the stretch from Steventon to Denchworth but a glance southward provides a reminder that the hills are not far off as the route runs parallel to the Berkshire Downs and a section of the Ridgeway. The flatness may prove a disadvantage to the cyclist as there is little protection from wind in this area so the going might be harder than you would have expected. A large section of the route overlaps part of the southern section of the Oxfordshire Cycleway.

The historic town of Wantage provides a pleasant stopping point. After Wantage there is a regrettable but largely unavoidable run on the A417 returning to Didcot. As A roads go, however, this one isn't too bad and this route provides a pleasant and fairly gentle introduction to the eastern section of the Vale of the White Horse.

Route

The first point of interest is to hand as soon as you step off the train. Signs in the station indicate the underground route to the Didcot Railway Centre. Step under...

Didcot Railway Centre

Definitely one for both the enthusiast and even for the mildly interested, the Railway Centre at Didcot commemorates the Golden Age of the Great Western Railway. Designed by Brunel, the railway between London and Bristol was completed in 1841. Nationalisation in 1948 put an end to the GWR's independence but the legend lives on. The Centre houses a collection of lovingly restored steam locomotives, a reconstruction of Brunel's original broad gauge trackwork and a replica of a country station.

The museum is open Saturday and Sunday all year, and most days from April to October, telephone 0235 817200.

When you've finished leave the station and turn left. Carry on for about 300 yards to the first turning on the left. Go under the railway bridge and the road will take you past a new housing estate and out onto the A4130. Turn right and then after about 300 yards turn left into the B4016 following the signs to Appleford, Sutton Courtenay and Drayton. At the end of the road turn left at the give way sign where there is a sign to Appleford one and a quarter miles and Sutton Courteney three and a quarter. Follow the road for nearly a mile when it veers to the right by the level crossing, bringing you close to Didcot's six great cooling towers of the coal fired power station. Built in the 1960s, they dominate the south Oxfordshire skyline, sending out continuous billowing clouds. They stand in stark contrast to the sleepy surrounding countryside.

Follow the road round to the right, past the level crossing towards Appleford. From Appleford veer left towards Sutton Courtenay which is just over a mile away.

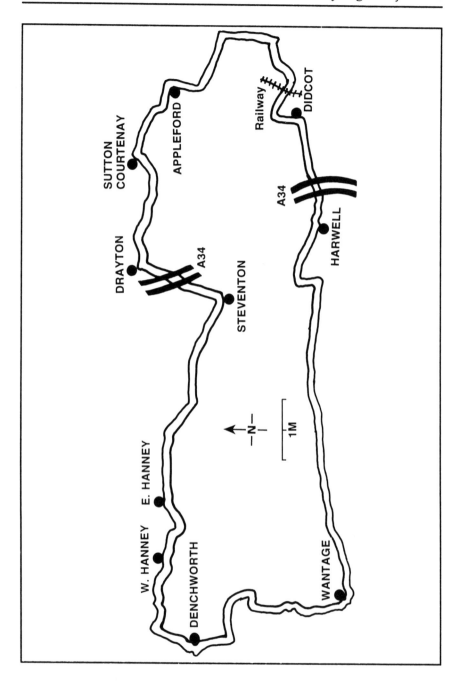

Sutton Courtenay

This picturesque village close to the Thames has a varied collection of substantial buildings including The Abbey which dates back to the 12th century and now serves as an interdenominational spiritual and retreat centre.

Also of note is the parish church yard (on your left as you ride into the village). It contains the grave of Herbert Henry Asquith, Earl of Oxford and Prime Minister from 1908 -1916. Also buried here in a simple grave is Eric Arthur Blair, better known as the writer George Orwell.

From Sutton Courtenay follow the road through the village and carry on for about one and a half miles to the mini roundabout at Drayton where you turn left to Steventon and into the B4017. The road takes you under the A34 and into Steventon. Look out for the sign to East Hanney three and a half miles and West Hanney four and a half and Grove six miles.

Turn right at the signs and the land now becomes flat and open with few signs of civilization as you cycle the three and a half miles to East Hanney, crossing over the A338. East Hanney reaches almost into West Hanney.

The Hanneys

The name "Hanney" means "island frequented by wild cocks". The island, (denoted by the suffix -ey) refers to an area of high ground above the surrounding swamps and streams of the Vale of the White Horse. In former times the Hanneys had a reputation for dampness and consequently unhealthiness. Eleanor G. Haydon, a local vicar's daughter, wrote the book "Islands of the Vale" (1908) depicting life in the area in a lost rural past.

From West Hanney veer left towards Denchworth. In the centre of Denchworth (it's a small village so you can't miss it) turn left at the sign Grove two and Wantage four miles. The road rises and falls slightly more and takes you over the railway bridge and into Grove.

Grove

Once a small agricultural community, Grove is now a rambling dormitory settlement. Most of the modern Grove has been built on a World War II airfield.

As you enter Grove, turn right at the give way sign, following the sign to Wantage Business Park one and a quarter and Wantage two and a quarter miles. The road takes you past the outskirts of Grove, veers left and then you turn right, still following the signs to Wantage. At the mini roundabout turn right and after about quarter of a mile turn right at the roundabout on the A338 following the signs to Wantage Town Centre.

Wantage

In this market town, on the foothills of the North Wessex Downs, Alfred the Great was born in 849 AD. The statue of Alfred in Wantage Market Square depicts him with an axe and scroll to commemorate his victory over the invading Danes and his restoration of education. The burnt cakes are tactfully not referred to.

Most of present day Wantage was built in the 17th and 18th century with the Stile Almshouses on Newbury Street dating back to 1690 – the courtyard here is cobbled with sheep's knuckle bones.

The Vale and Downland Museum Centre in The Old Surgery in Church Street is well worth a visit. The museum tells the history of life in the Vale from the Ice Age. There are frequent exhibitions and a cafe here.

Leave Wantage from the town centre via the A417, following the signs to Didcot. A series of mini roundabouts will bring you to the edge of the town and from here there is a straight ride of about four miles to the roundabout at Rowstock Corner. Turn left here into the A4130, following the signs to Didcot. Take the first turning right at the sign to Harwell village (this is one mile through Milton Hill Orchards). Turn left at the junction and follow the road round to the right. This is the B4493 which will take you into Didcot. Cross over the railway bridge and cycle for about one mile to the roundabout where you turn left, following the signs to the station. At the next roundabout turn right and the station is about 500 yards on the left.

King Alfred the Great's statue, Wantage

Route 19:
Swindon – Uffington – Fernham – Swindon

Distance: 32 miles.

Not many opportunities to cut this short without missing out places of interest. You could by-pass Kingston Lisle and go to Uffington via Woolstone. There are several ways of lengthening this route – you can continue past the Blowing Stone to Wantage and link with Route 18.

Maps: Ordnance Survey Landranger 173 and 174. A town map for Swindon would also be helpful for this route.

Rail Access: The journey starts and finishes at Swindon Station.

Tourist Information: Swindon, 32 The Arcade, Brunel Centre, Vale and Downland Centre in Wantage can offer useful information on the region.

Cycle Shops: Grove Auto Spares and Cycles, Grove.

Special Interest: The White Horse, Uffington Castle, Wayland's Smithy, Dragon Hill, The Blowing Stone, Kingston Lisle Park, Uffington Museum.

Refreshments: The White Horse at Woolstone, The Blowing Stone Inn at Kingston Lisle, several pubs and shops on route.

General Description

This route takes in Oxfordshire's western section of the Vale of the White Horse. An unfortunate lack of public transport in the area means that the journey begins over the border in Swindon in Wiltshire and there is a fair amount of urban traffic to negotiate at the beginning and end of the route. That said, this journey is well worth any inconveniences, being rich in natural beauty and ancient monuments – not least the White Horse itself. Running parallel to the Ridgeway, the first half of the route rises and falls – not too steeply – and winds against the backdrop of hills to the south and the low lying plains stretching for miles to the north. The return journey takes you through this flatter part of the Vale.

Route

From Swindon Station turn left and carry straight ahead until you reach the first roundabout (at the second railway bridge). Turn right here into the busy A4259. Stay on this road for about three and a half miles, carrying straight over what seems like countless roundabouts until you reach the final big one at the junction with the A419 where you will see the sign to Wanborough. Carry straight over leaving the A road for the minor road to Wanborough. You now begin to get a clearer view of the Ridgeway and Downs to your right.

A long rise will bring you into the village of Wanborough where you carry straight through to the give way sign at the crossroads. Go straight over, following the sign to Hinton Parva, Bishopstone and Ashbury. Pass through these villages as the road winds and descends through the Vale. When you reach the give way sign at the junction at Ashbury you can carry straight over into the B4507 or turn right here, following the sign to Wayland's Smithy via the B4000 and turning left along the Ridgeway or, alternately carry straight on along the B4507 until you see a sign right which takes you on a steep climb to the Smithy.

Wayland's Smithy

This is an ancient burial chamber which dates back about 5,000 years and is the oldest of the many monuments in this area. Excavations between 1962 – 1963 revealed that two successive neolithic barrows had been built one over the other. The remains of at least fourteen individuals were found in the first tomb and eight in the second.

The legend about Wayland the Smith dates back to Saxon times and is first mentioned in a Saxon charter of 955 AD. As with all legends there are several versions but the most enduring one is Sir Walter Scott's. According to Scott, the Ridgeway traveller who ties up his horse to a stone puts down a coin on a flat stone and looks the other way for ten minutes will find his horse shod and the money gone. I don't know if it would work for a bicycle puncture.

The Ridgeway

This eighty-five mile long distance path stretches from Avebury in Wiltshire to Ivinghoe Beacon in Hertfordshire. It dates back 5,000 years and is Britain's oldest pathway (and possibly the world's).

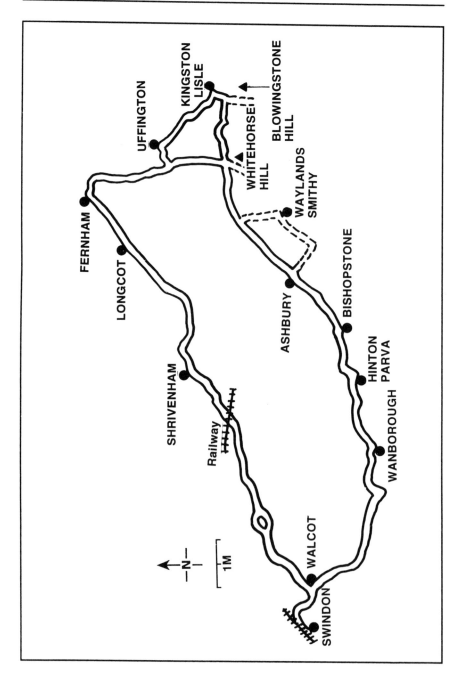

From the Smithy return down to the B4507 and turn right. Carry on for about three quarters of a mile until you see the sign right to the White Horse and left to Woolstone Lodge Tavern where you may want to refresh yourself before a long haul up to the White Horse up Woolstone Hill for about half a mile (but feels much longer).

The White Horse

This White Horse figure cut into the chalk hillside below Uffington Castle is believed to be the first of all the hill figures in Britain and is certainly the most well known.

The origin and function of the Horse are a mystery. Popular legend claimed that it was cut to celebrate the victory of King Alfred at the battle of Ashdown in 871 AD but this is no more than speculation. There is a reference to the hill of the White Horse in an 11th century document of Abingdon Abbey and in the 14th century it was described as second only to Stonehenge as a marvel of Britain.

The horse owes its whiteness to the chalk rock of the north facing scarp slope of the downs. It is 360ft long and 130ft tall. The sharp sided valley below the White Horse is known as the Manger. Given the Horse's size a hefty feeding ground might seem appropriate but in fact the name Manger probably indicates a Saxon trading centre and the link with the Horse is purely a popular association.

There are many popular superstitions surrounding the horse the best known being that if you stand in its eye you can make a wish. The English Heritage Society, whose care it is in, would probably prefer it if you didn't.

Further up from the White Horse is Uffington Castle.

Uffington Castle

This is an Iron Age hill fort where burial sites of the Anglo-Saxon and Roman period have been found. It dates back to about the first century BC and is surrounded by a defensive bank and ditch.

When you've finished return to the B4507 road and turn right. Continue with the full view of the White Horse on your right to Dragon's Hill at the crossroads to Uffington

Dragon's Hill

Found on the east side of the manger, there is a persistent tradition that it was here that St George slew the dragon. The bare ground is supposed to be where the dragon's blood was shed. This legend has sparked off further speculation in recent times that the White Horse may be the steed of St George.

At Dragon's Hill turn left to Uffington or you can lengthen the route by carrying on for about a mile and a half to the Blowing Stone. Turn right at the next crossroads opposite Kingston Lisle.

The Blowing Stone

300 yards on your left at Blowing Stone Hill is this large Saracen stone which is a natural amplifier of sound. The wind blowing through a hole in the stone is said to produce a noise like a fog horn which will carry a great distance. Legend (another one) says that King Alfred called his troops to battle by using the blowing stone. Thomas Hughes, author of "Tom Brown's Schooldays" who lived in nearby Uffington, writes of the stone that it made a "gruesome sound between a moan and a roar" and had a "ghost-like awful voice" which could be heard from seven miles around.

From the Blowing Stone cross over the B4507 to Kingston Lisle where you can visit Kingston Lisle Park.

Kingston Lisle Park

This was once the home of Lord Raglan, Commander-in-Chief in the Crimean War. The house was built in 1677 with additions in the early 19th century. It contains a collection of Raglan's letters, 17th century glass, needlework and carpets designed by the Pre-Raphaelite William Morris. There is also the park to wander round. Limited opening times, telephone 036782223.

From Kingston Lisle follow the road to Uffington about one and three quarter miles.

Uffington

The most distinctive feature of Uffington is the octagonal tower of St Mary's Church once, rather pretentiously, know as the Cathedral of the Vale of the White Horse. Inside the Church is a bronze memorial to Uffington's most famous inhabitant – Thomas Hughes. As well as "Tom Brown's School Days", Hughes wrote extensively of the social history and customs of Uffington and he is commemorated in the village museum – Tom Brown's School Museum on Broad Street, telephone 0367 820 675.

Go through Uffington and look for the sign north to Fernham. There is now an easy flat ride to Fernham of about two miles. Veer left towards the village, joining the B4508 and follow the signs to Longcot. Just past this small village carry straight on, leaving the B4508 for the minor road past the Royal Military College of Science and through the village of Shrivenham. From here veer right, following the signs to Swindon and the A420. Ride with care along the A420, heading for Swindon Town Centre (about five miles away). Negotiate the large roundabout on the outskirts with caution and join the A4312 which will bring you to the roundabout at Walcot where you turn right and follow the signs for the centre and station.

Route 20:
Oxfordshire Cycleway

Note: Recommended for this route is the Oxfordshire County Council's map (cost 50p) of the Oxfordshire Cycleway, available from Oxford Town Hall, Oxford Tourist information and various cycle shops in the city and county (see under appendix at end of book).

General Information

This 200 mile Cycleway roughly traces the border around Oxfordshire and followed on from the success of the long-distance Cycleway in neighbouring Wiltshire. It became official in 1990 under the aegis of the County Council's Department of Arts and Leisure in response to demand from cyclists. The route is sign posted throughout by distinctive blue and white signs with arrows, a bicycle and the words "Oxfordshire Cycleway", and there are signposts for the anti-clockwise route as well as the clockwise one. The route is circular and can be joined at any point but there is a linking route from Burford through Oxford City to Horton-cum-Studley. This route is known as the Windrush Valley route and is highlighted on the City Council's Oxfordshire Cycleway map. For the most part the route follows quiet country lanes with a minimum of time spent on busy roads. Several sections of the route are hilly, encompassing as it does the Chiltern Hills, North Wessex Downs and the Oxfordshire Cotswolds. From Goring to White Horse Hill you can also opt for the alternative Ridgeway Route – see Council Map for details.

It is possible to do the route in small slices over several weekends and the nearest railway stations have been indicated with this in mind. That said, nothing quite compares with completing the whole Cycleway in one go and you are better able to appreciate the changing landscape as you continually ride through it (you also gain an incredibly smug feeling at the end of it).

Places of interest: to avoid duplication, information on the various places to visit are not included in this section if they have already been described elsewhere in this guide.

Practicalities: If you're new to longer distance cycling a number of factors need to be born in mind when attempting the Cycleway. They are mainly common sense but ignoring them could take away some of the pleasure of the journey.

Pacing it: Plan the amount of miles you do in a day carefully so that it is within your capabilities. Be prepared to use low gears, go slowly and to stop and rest at regular intervals. Bear in mind also that you may be carrying a heavier load than usual which will slow you down. Whilst not essential, a wide selection of gears will make the journey more comfortable and easier to complete.

Food and Drink: Nearly all of this route is on quiet country roads where shops are few and far between so remember to stock up adequately when the opportunity presents itself. The Cycleway by-passes towns on all sections of the route.

Maps: Whilst all of the route is signposted you will almost certainly have to deviate from the main route to find accommodation, stations etc. Additionally, until you get used to it it's easy to miss the blue arrows so good maps are important. Whilst you can manage the route solely on the Council's Oxfordshire Cycleway map, good maps (such as the ordnance survey maps) will make the journey easier. Maps covering this route are: Ordnance Survey Landranger 151, 164, 165, 174 and 175.

Accommodation: If you are doing the whole route or a substantial section of it you will need to arrange overnight accommodation. Information on this can be obtained from the Tourist Information Centres indicated on each section and also from the list of useful publications at the end of this book. The Cyclists Touring Club (see appendix) also provides a list of accommodation addresses for each county which is available to members. I have indicated Youth hostels on route. It sounds obvious but it is better to make arrangements in advance rather than turn up hopefully on the door.

Note: The basic distance for this route is 200 miles but you will need to make deviations for public transport and accommodation *en route* which will increase the mileage.

I describe here the clockwise route starting from Oxford City and joining the official route at Horton-cum-Studley. This is largely for convenience and because it coincides with that given on the Council's Oxfordshire Cycleway map. You can join the route anywhere on the circuit.

Oxfordshire Cycleway – Part 1

Route: Oxford – Horton-cum-Studley – Thame – Goring.

Distance: (approximate) 50 miles.

Maps: Ordnance Survey Landranger 164, 165 and 175.

Rail Access: Railway Stations at Oxford, Henley, and Goring.

Tourist Information: Oxford, St Aldates, Thame, Town Hall, High Street, Henley-on-Thames, Town Hall, Market Place.

Cycle Shops: See Appendix under Oxford Cycle Shops.

Thame Cycles, 69a Park Street, Thame, Hammonds, Bell Street, Henley.

Special Interest: Stonor Park (Stonor), Grey's Court (Henley), The Maharaja's Well (Stoke Row).

Refreshments: Pubs and shops in Thame and Henley, tea rooms at Stonor, shops at Goring.

Youth Hostel: Goring/Streatley.

Links with other Routes: Routes 7, 8, 9 and 10.

General Description

Starting in Oxford, this section of the Cycleway follows the eastern section of the Windrush Valley route (see above), joining the Oxfordshire Cycleway at Horton-cum-Studley. The first part of this section is fairly easy, crossing low lying farmland of east Oxford, through the town of Thame before approaching the foothills of the Chilterns and crossing over the Ridgeway. The long steep climb through the wooded hills of the Chilterns is the start of many but the views are correspondingly attractive. By-passing Henley (which is well worth a detour) the route veers west. Of particular interest and directly on the route is the Maharaja's Well at Stoke Row and this section of the Cycleway ends on a refreshing downhill ride into the attractive riverside towns of Goring and Streatley, astride the River Thames.

Route

From Carfax tower in the City Centre follow the High Street to the end and veer left at The Plain roundabout. This takes you into St Clements and the A420 where you turn left at the second set of traffic lights into Marston Road and the B4150. At the end of Marston Road dog leg left at the roundabout and then right at the second roundabout, still following the B4150. Follow the road over the A40 and turn right towards Elsfield. Carry on to the junction at the B4027 where you dog leg left and right to Beckley and Horton-cum-Studley.

At Horton-cum-Studley you join the Oxfordshire cycleway (look out for the distinctive blue and white signs). From here, follow the signs to Worminghall, Ickford and Shabbington, which takes you temporarily over the border into Buckinghamshire. Go through Shabbington, crossing the River Thame back into Oxfordshire and turn left at the junction of the A418 to Thame. Follow the road and signs with care to the roundabout and carry straight over to Thame (see Route 7).

Carry on through Thame's main street, looking for signs to the B4445. Go straight on for about two and a half miles and turn off right here towards Sydenham. Past Sydenham turn left to Kingston Blount where you dog leg sharp right and left across the B4009. The road now takes you across the Ridgeway and to the foothills of the Chilterns. Be prepared for a major climb through Kingston Wood to the A40. Dog leg left and right here and follow the road over the M40 towards Christmas Common. There is a picnic site and an Oxfordshire Sculpture Project with a Sculpture Trail here at Cowleaze Wood on your left run by the Forestry Commission. Follow the road to the crossroad at Christmas Common where you veer left and follow the bridle path, passing by Northend and Turville Heath where you veer right towards the B480. At the B480, veer left to Stonor (see Route 9).

Past Stonor Estate, look out for the turn right to Russell's Water Common. Follow the hill up to the Common and look out for the bridleway left to Bix Botton. This brings you out into the little village of Bix next to the A423. If you want to visit nearby Henley-on-Thames (see ride 10) you can make a detour here turning left along the A423 and proceed with CARE to Henley town centre. From Henley, return the way you came and look out for the sign off to the left opposite Bix.

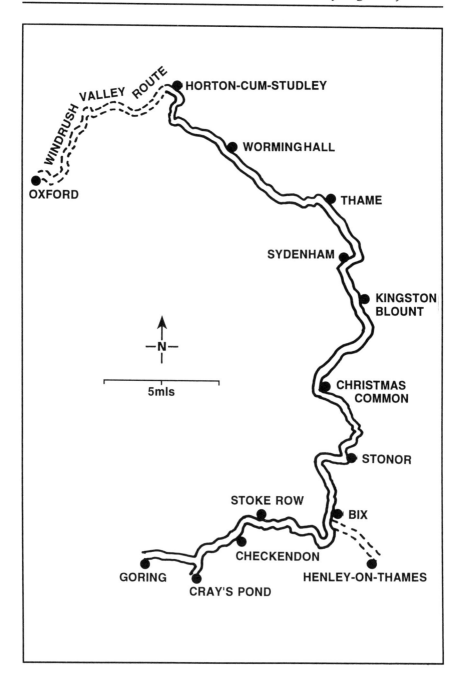

WINDRUSH VALLEY ROUTE

HORTON-CUM-STUDLEY

WORMINGHALL

OXFORD

THAME

SYDENHAM

KINGSTON BLOUNT

—N—

5mls

CHRISTMAS COMMON

STONOR

STOKE ROW

BIX

CHECKENDON

GORING

CRAY'S POND

HENLEY-ON-THAMES

From Bix Bottom, cross the dual carriage way of the A423 with Great Care and follow the road as it veers left to Lambridge wood and past Grey's Court on your right (see ride 10).

From Grey's Court look out for the narrow track right which takes you up through woodland to the B481 where you turn right towards Highmoor Cross. Turn left at Highmoor Cross towards Stoke Row. At Stoke Row you will find the Maharaja's Well on your right along the main street (see Ride 8 for details).

Pass through Stoke Row and turn left to Checkendon. Follow the road to the A4074. Dog leg right then left with care towards Woodcote. At Woodcote turn left at the crossroads at the B471. Before you reach Cray's Pond look out for the sign right which takes you on a nice easy descent through Cleeve to Goring and the B4009. Turn left here for the station and Youth hostel.

Oxfordshire Cycleway – Part 2

Route: Goring – Wallingford – Wantage – Buscot.

Distance: (approximate) 50 miles.

Maps: Ordnance Survey Landranger 175, 164, 174, 163.

Rail Access: Stations at Goring and Didcot (also off the route at Swindon).

Tourist Information: Wallingford 9 St Martin's Street, The Vale and Downland Museum in Wantage offers information on areas of local interest, Swindon, 32 The Arcade, Brunel Centre.

Cycle Shops: Castles of Wallingford, St Mary's Street Wallingford; Dentons Cycles, 133 The Broadway, Didcot; Grove Auto Spares and Cycles, 9 Millbrook Square, Grove; A.L. Vickers at Drayton sells cycle spares.

Special Interest: Wallingford Castle and Museum, Didcot Railway Centre, Wantage Vale and Downland Museum, The White Horse, Wayland's Smithy, Uffington Castle, the Blowing Stone, Dragon's Hill Uffington museum, St John's Lock.

Refreshments: Shops, cafes and restaurants in Wallingford, Didcot and Wantage, The Trout Inn at St John's Lock.

Youth Hostel: The Court Hill Ridgeway Centre, Court Hill, Wantage.

Links with other Routes: Routes 9, 18, 19.

General Description

The first part of the route from Goring to Sutton Courtenay runs roughly parallel to the River Thames. The backdrop of the Chilterns and the Ridgeway around Goring provides scenery which is magnificent in places. Beyond Didcot the route takes a flattish journey through the Vale of the White Horse. Past Wantage it runs closely parallel to the Ridgeway and is correspondingly hilly – again, the hills provide a splendid backdrop and the area is rich in prehistoric monuments, giving it a timeless, haunting feel. Close to the White Horse Monument the route turns north towards Farringdon, leading to one of the best preserved tithe barns in the country at Great Coxwell. This section of the journey ends back at the River Thames at Buscot, much closer to its source now. Just across the border in Wiltshire is the lovely little town of Lechlade. St John's Lock, between Lechlade and Buscott, is the furthest navigable point for powered craft on the river and the Trout Inn by the lock is renowned for its excellent fish dishes.

Route

At Goring follow the B4009 which runs adjacent to sections of the Ridgeway towards Wallingford. Go past the villages of South and North Stoke and past Carmel College (Britain's only Jewish public school) on your left. The road merges into the A4074 until the roundabout where you turn left into the A4130 through Crowmarsh Gifford, across the river Thames into Wallingford (see Route 9).

From Wallingford follow the A4130 and look out for the sign left to Brightwell-cum-Sotwell (home of the famous Bach Flower Remedies). Ride through this pleasant village to the A4130 again and dog leg right and left onto a minor road which brings you to the B4016 to Appleford and the not so glorious view of Didcot Power Station on your left. Although the route by-passes Didcot you may want to pay a visit to the Didcot railway centre which is based at the Railway Station. The museum is open Saturday and Sunday all year, and most days from April to October, telephone 0235 817200. (See Route 18)

Follow the route to Appleford where you veer left at the village green and follow the road to the attractive village of Sutton Courtenay. Pay a visit to the churchyard where you will find the graves of Lord Asquith (British Prime Minister from 1908 – 1916) and George Orwell, buried under his real name, Eric Blair. Follow the road through Sutton Courtenay to Drayton where you turn left into the B4017 to Steventon. Go under the A34 and at Steventon look out for the sign right to East Hanney, West Hanney and Denchworth. Turn right here into the open flat land in the eastern section of the Vale of the White Horse.

Pass through the villages of East and West Hanney and at Denchworth follow the road to Grove, crossing over the railway. There's nothing much of interest in Grove but here is a good opportunity to visit the historic town of Wantage. Follow the signs from Grove. (See Route 18 for Wantage).

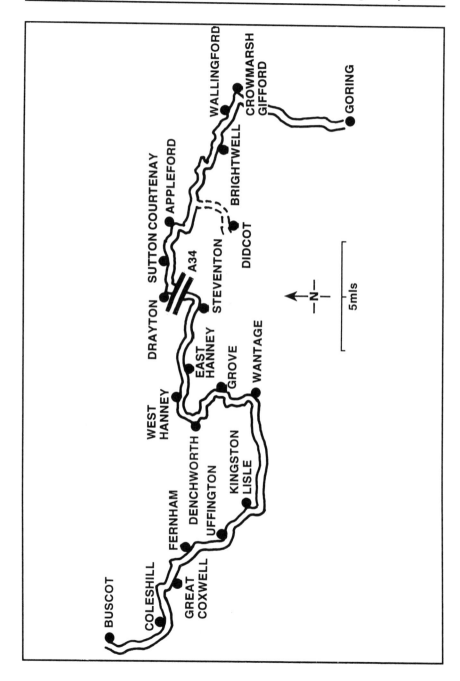

Leave Wantage via the B4507 which takes you east past the villages of Childrey, Sparsholt and Kingston Lisle. This is a hilly route but offers beautiful scenery of the Ridgeway on your left and the lower land of the Vale stretching away on your right. Beyond Kingston Lisle the route turns off right towards Uffington but if you've got the energy there are several fascinating monuments to explore on the hillsides.

When you've finished head back along the B4507 to the turn off for Kingston Lisle and Uffington. You may want to visit Kingston Lisle Park.

From Kingston Lisle follow the road to Uffington with its striking octagonal church and a small museum devoted to the author Thomas Hushes on Broad Street. From Uffington follow the route to Fernham, crossing the B4508 and heading to Little Coxwell. Cross over the busy A420 with care, go through Great Coxwell and veer right towards the Great Barn.

The Great Barn

Owned by the National Trust, this tithe barn probably dates back to the mid-13th century. At 152ft long, 44ft wide and 48ft high, it is an impressive structure and is generally considered to be one of the best examples of a surviving medieval barn in the country.

Carry on to the B4019 where you turn left. Go past Badbury hill on your right (also owned by the National Trust) and carry on to Coleshill where you turn right again. The long straight road leads you to the A417 running parallel to the Thames. At the junction, close to Buscot turn left. After about three quarters of a mile you come to St John's Bridge and St John's Lock close to the Trout Inn.

St John's Lock

This is the highest lock on the Thames and here you will find the reclining statue of "Old Father Thames". The statue was originally carved for the Crstal Palace exhibition, and was rescued from the subsequent ruins and transported to the the source of the Thames near Cirencester. It had to be rescued again because of vandalism and has finally come to rest at St John's Lock.

Oxfordshire Cycleway – Part 3

Route: Buscot – Burford – Chipping Norton – Banbury.

Distance: (approximately) 60 miles.

Maps: Ordnance Survey 163, 164, 151.

Rail Access: Stations at Charlbury, (Shipton under Wychwood has very limited services), Kingham, Banbury.

Tourist Information: Witney, Town Hall, Market Square, Burford, The Brewery, Sheep Street, Banbury, 8 Horsefair.

Cycle Shops: Giles Cycles, 1 Alvescot Road, Carterton; Dentons, 1 High Street, Witney; Banbury Cycles Ltd, 54 Bridge Street; Banbury Garden Machinery, 2 Bridge Street;Trinders, 56– 59 Broad Street, Banbury.

Special Interest: Kelmscott Manor, Tolsey Museum (Burford), The Rollright Stones (Chipping Norton), Banbury Museum.

Refreshments: Burford pubs, tea shops and restaurants, ditto Chipping Norton and Banbury.

Youth Hostel: Charlbury.

Links with other Routes: Routes 13, 14, 15 and 16.

General Information

This section of the route takes you northwards into the Oxfordshire Cotswolds. Just beyond Buscot is Kelmscott – home to William Morris the pre-Raphaelite painter. From here there are a number of attractive villages built in greyish stone which gradually takes on the mellow golden hue that is characteristic of the Cotswolds. The route by-passes the attractive town of Burford (well worth a quick visit via the Windrush Valley route) and takes you through the patchwork hills of classic Cotswold scenery – there is a fair amount of climbing in this section and it includes Oxfordshire's highest town at Chipping Norton. Just beyond Chipping Norton are the prehistoric Rollright stones and then the route takes you to Oxfordshire's most northern town at Banbury.

Route

From the A417 take the turn right at the sign to Kelmscott just beyond the Trout Inn. The route by-passes Kelmscott but this is certainly worth a quick diversion. Look out for the signs on the right to Kelmscott village and go straight through to the Manor which is at the end.

Kelmscott

This grey stone Elizabethan manor was the home of the pre-Raphaelite, William Morris. Morris used it as a country home between 1871 and 1896, occasionally sharing it with fellow pre-Raphaelite Dante Gabriel Rossetti. A man of many talents (painter, craftsman, writer and socialist), Morris is perhaps better known today for his wallpaper designs. In his book "News from Nowhere" (1892) he describes the house. The house is owned by the London Society of Antiquaries and contains collections of Morris's works and those of his associates. Morris is buried in Kelmscott churchyard. Limited Opening Times (currently only on Wednesdays from April to September), Telephone 0367 252486 for details.

Leave Kelmscott and return to the route where you follow the signs to Langford. At Langford turn right at the Crown Pub to Broadwell and Kencott where you turn right then left, by-passing the unprepossessing town of Carterton, towards Shilton. Turn right towards Shilton and the B4020. Cross over the B4020 and the road will bring you out onto the A40 near Burford. Dog leg left and right with Great Care across the A40 and enjoy the ride down to the lovely village of Swinbrook on the river Windrush.

You can make a diversion here, however, by turning left and following the Windrush Valley Cycle Route which will bring you out into the centre of Burford (see Route 13).

When you've finished in Burford retrace the journey back to Swinbrook and begin climbing through the beautiful Cotswold scenery towards Shipton under Wychwood. Veer left here towards the A361. Follow the road through Milton under Wychwood towards Bruern Abbey where you veer right, crossing over the railway to the junction. Turn left here and follow the road to the end where it joins the B4450. Turn left and take the first turn left to Kingham and go through Kingham and carry on to the crossroads where you turn right to Cornwell. Go through the

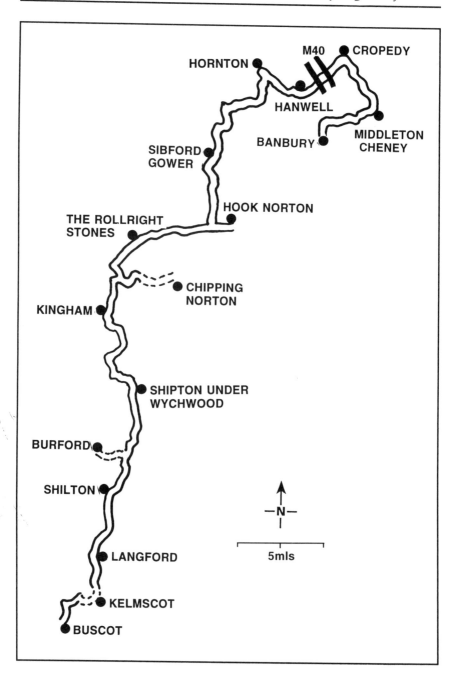

village and follow the road and turn left to the A44 where you can divert to Chipping Norton (see Route 14).

You can join the route from Chipping Norton by going through the town and turning left at the end of the main street, following the signs to the Rollright stones and Great Rollright. If you have not diverted to Chipping Norton dog leg left and right at the A44 and the road will take you to the Rollright Stones (see Route 14).

From here carry on to the A3400 in the noperson's land between the Warwickshire and the Oxfordshire border. Cross over and enjoy the lovely views to the left. Carry on to the right turning through Church End. Go past Church End and then turn left to Hook Norton with its attractive stone houses and famous (locally) brewery. From Hook Norton follow the route through Sibford Gower then turn left into the B4035, following the signs to Epwell. From Epwell follow the road to the junction where you turn left, carry on for about one mile and then turn right to Shennington and Alkerton. Go straight through Alkerton to the junction at the A422 and turn right here then left following the steep descent and sharp rise through the village of Hornton. At the top turn right towards Horley (enjoy the plateau). At Horley turn left towards the B4100 where you dog leg right and left towards Hanwell. After Hanwell carry straight on over the M40 to the A423 where you turn left then right to Great Bourton. Past Great Bouton carry on under the railway bridge into Cropedy and the most northern Point of the route.

At Cropedy, turn right over the canal towards Williamscot. Just beyond Williamscot is the A361 where you turn right then left towards Chacombe, temporarily border hopping into Northamptonshire. From Chacombe veer left towards Middleton Cheney. Here cross over the B4525 and turn right towards the A422. Cross over, going left towards Overthorpe. Turn right towards Banbury. Carry straight into Banbury Town Centre crossing over the M40 again. The Railway Station is on your left and straight ahead is the Town Centre (see Route 15 for Banbury).

Oxfordshire Cycleway – Part 4

Route: Banbury – Upper Heyford – Islip – Horton-cum-Studley – Oxford.

Distance (approximately): 40 miles.

Maps: Ordnance Survey Landranger 151, 164.

Rail Access: Station at Banbury, Limited train services to Bicester and Lower Heyford (check for details).

Tourist Information: Banbury, 8 Horsefair.

Cycle Shops: Banbury Cycles Ltd, 54 Bridge Street; Banbury Garden Machinery, 2 Bridge Street; Trinders, 56 – 59 Broad Street, Banbury, Deddington; The Cyclogical Shop, Garage Courtyard, Hudson Street, Bicester; Broadribbs 83 – 85 Sheep Street.

Special Interest: Broughton Castle, Bloxham Museum.

Refreshments: Banbury shops, tea shops, restaurants otherwise fairly limited on this route.

Youth Hostel: Oxford.

Links with Other Routes: Routes 4 and 17.

General Description

This last stretch of the Cycleway brings you full circle northwards back to Oxford. The cycling is on the whole gentler down the eastern side of the County. The route goes through the valley of the river Cherwell and the area around Somerton and Upper Heyford is particularly attractive. Further south the route skirts around the low lying fenland of Otmoor before bringing you into Horton-cum-Studley and the route back to Oxford.

Route

From Banbury Tourist information carry straight on past the Banbury Cross into the B4035 road which takes you into open country to the

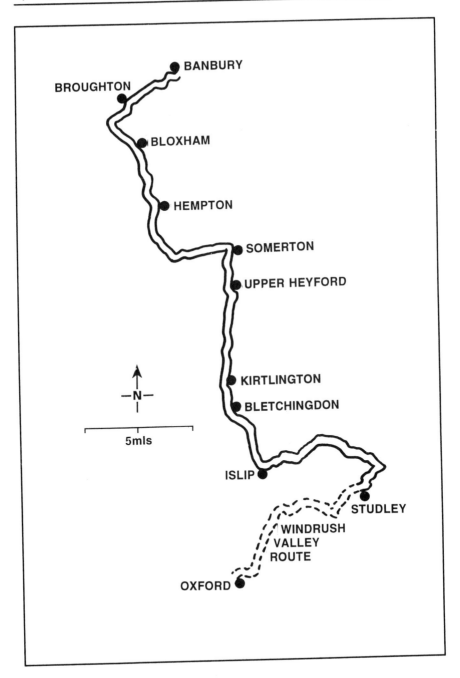

village of Broughton. At the Saye and Sele Arms turn right to visit Broughton Castle (see Route 15).

From Broughton carry straight on to Lower Tadmarton. From here turn left to Bloxham where you can visit Bloxham museum in the Old Court House which reflects past life in the village. From Bloxham cross the A361 towards Barford St John and Barford St Michael. At Barford St Michael veer left towards the B4031 at Hempton. Cross straight over towards the pretty village of Duns Tew. From here veer left towards North Aston. Cross over the A4260 with care into North Aston and descend towards the River Cherwell and Canal. Cross over both and under the railway bridge to Somerton where you veer right uphill towards Upper Heyford. Enjoy the views over the valley to your right. In Upper Heyford the route turns left with the eerie US airbase on your left. Turn right for a nice, straight stretch, cross over the B4030 towards Kirtlington where you temporarily join the A4095 and leave it for Bletchingdon, turning left out of Kirtlington. From Bletchingdon carry on along the B4027 to Islip, a pretty village set on the River Ray where Edward the Confessor was born. From Islip follow the signs to Otmoor passing through the villages of Oddington, Charlton, Fencott and Murcott (see Route 4 for Otmoor).

Over the M40 at Boarstall, veer right towards Horton-cum-Studley thus completing the circle. You can now follow the road back to Oxford via Beckley.

Appendix

Useful Addresses

General

The Cyclists Touring Club (CTC)
Cotterell House
69 Meadrow
Godalming
Surrey GU7 3HS

The Youth Hostel Association
Trevelyan House
8 St Stephens Hill
St Albans
Herts AL1 2DY

Maps

Ordnance Survey, Dept IC
Romsey Road
Maybush
Southampton SO9 4DH

Useful Addresses in Oxford

Tourist Information Centre
St Aldates
Oxford
Tel: (0865) 726871

Thames Valley Police
Cycles Department
Floyds Row (off St Aldates)
Oxford OX1 1SZ
Tel: (0865) 266280

Cyclox
The East Oxford Community Centre
Princes Street
Oxford OX4 1DD

Oxford City Council
Department of Engineering and Recreation
Town Hall
St Aldates
Oxford OX1 1BX
Cycling Officers: (0865) 252405

Oxford City Cycle Shops (a few!)

Bee-line Bicycles
61 – 63 Cowley Road
Oxford

Warlands*
(Botley Road Cycles)
63 Botley Road
Oxford

Broadribbs*
6 Lincoln House
Market Street
Oxford

Dentons Cycles*
294 Banbury Road
Oxford

Pennyfarthing Cycles*
5 George Street
Oxford

Les Smith
7 Prama House
267 Banbury Road
Oxford

Spokes Cycles
319 Abingdon Road
Oxford

Walton Street Cycles
78 Walton Street
Oxford

* These shops also hire bicycles

We publish a wide range of other titles, including general interest publications, guides to individual towns, and books for outdoor activities centred on walking and cycling in the great outdoors throughout England and Wales. This is a recent selection:

Cycling with Sigma

CYCLE UK! The Essential Guide to Leisure Cycling
- Les Lumsdon *(£9.95)*

OFF-BEAT CYCLING & MOUNTAIN BIKING IN THE PEAK DISTRICT
- Clive Smith *(£6.95)*

***MORE* OFF-BEAT CYCLING IN THE PEAK DISTRICT**
- Clive Smith *(£6.95)*

50 BEST CYCLE RIDES IN CHESHIRE
- edited by Graham Beech *(£7.95)*

CYCLING IN THE LAKE DISTRICT
- John Wood *(£7.95)*

CYCLING IN SOUTH WALES
- Rosemary Evans *(£7.95)*

CYCLING IN THE COTSWOLDS
- Stephen Hill *(£7.95)*

CYCLING IN NORTH STAFFORDSHIRE
- Linda Wain *(£7.95)*

BY-WAY BIKING IN THE CHILTERNS
- Henry Tindell *(£7.95)*

Peak District Walks

HERITAGE WALKS IN THE PEAK DISTRICT - Clive Price *(£6.95)*

CHALLENGING WALKS IN NORTH-WEST BRITAIN - Ron Astley *(£7.95)*

WALKING PEAKLAND TRACKWAYS - Mike Cresswell *(£7.95)*

MOSTLY DOWNHILL, Leisurely Walks - White Peak - Clive Price *(£6.95)*

MOSTLY DOWNHILL, Leisurely Walks - Dark Peak - Clive Price *(£6.95)*

Country Walking . . .

RAMBLES IN NORTH WALES - Roger Redfern

EAST CHESHIRE WALKS - Graham Beech

WEST CHESHIRE WALKS - Jen Darling

WEST PENNINE WALKS - Mike Cresswell

STAFFORDSHIRE WALKS - Les Lumsdon

NEWARK AND SHERWOOD RAMBLES - Malcolm McKenzie

NORTH NOTTINGHAMSHIRE RAMBLES - Malcolm McKenzie

RAMBLES AROUND NOTTINGHAM & DERBY - Keith Taylor

RAMBLES AROUND MANCHESTER - Mike Cresswell

WESTERN LAKELAND RAMBLES - Gordon Brown *(£5.95)*

WELSH WALKS: Dolgellau and the Cambrian Coast
- Laurence Main and Morag Perrott *(£5.95)*

WELSH WALKS: Aberystwyth and District
- Laurence Main and Morag Perrott *(£5.95)*

WEST PENNINE WALKS - Mike Cresswell

TEASHOP WALKS IN THE CHILTERNS — Jean Patefield

WATERWAY WALKS AROUND BIRMINGHAM — David Perrott

- all of the above books are currently £6.95 each, except where indicated

Long-distance walks:

THE GREATER MANCHESTER BOUNDARY WALK - Graham Phythian

THE THIRLMERE WAY - Tim Cappelli

THE FURNESS TRAIL - Tim Cappelli

THE MARCHES WAY - Les Lumsdon

THE TWO ROSES WAY - Peter Billington, Eric Slater, Bill Greenwood and Clive Edwards

THE RED ROSE WALK - Tom Schofield

FROM WHARFEDALE TO WESTMORLAND:
historical walks through the Yorkshire Dales - Aline Watson

THE WEST YORKSHIRE WAY - Nicholas Parrott

- all £6.95 each

The Best Pub Walks!

Sigma publish the widest range of "Pub Walks" guides, covering just about every popular walking destination in England and Wales. Each book includes 25 - 30 interesting walks and varied suitable for individuals or family groups. *The walks are based on "Real Ale" inns of character and are all accessible by public transport.*

Areas covered include

Cheshire • Dartmoor • Exmoor • Isle of Wight • Yorkshire Dales • Peak District • Pennines • Lake District • Cotswolds • Mendips • Cornwall • Lancashire • Oxfordshire • Snowdonia • Devon • Northumbria • Snowdonia • Manchester

... and dozens more - all £6.95 each!

General interest:

THE INCREDIBLY BIASED BEER GUIDE - Ruth Herman

This is the most comprehensive guide to Britain's smaller breweries and the pubs where you can sample their products. Produced with the collaboration of the Small Independent Brewers' Association and including a half-price subscription to The Beer Lovers' Club. *£6.95*

DIAL 999 - EMERGENCY SERVICES IN ACTION - John Creighton

Re-live the excitement as fire engines rush to disasters. See dramatic rescues on land and sea. Read how the professionals keep a clear head and swing into action. **£6.95**

THE ALABAMA AFFAIR - David Hollett

This is an account of Britain's rôle in the American Civil War. Read how Merseyside dockyards supplied ships for the Confederate navy, thereby supporting the slave trade. The *Alabama* was the most famous of the 'Laird Rams', and was chased half way across the world before being sunk ignominiously. *£6.95*

PEAK DISTRICT DIARY - Roger Redfern

An evocative book, celebrating the glorious countryside of the Peak District. The book is based on Roger's popular column in *The Guardian* newspaper and is profusely illustrated with stunning photographs. *£6.95*

I REMAIN, YOUR SON JACK - J. C. Morten (edited by Sheila Morten)

A collection of almost 200 letters, as featured on BBC TV, telling the moving story of a young soldier in the First World War. Profusely illustrated with contemporary photographs. *£8.95*

FORGOTTEN DIVISIONS - John Fox

A unique account of the 1914 - 18 War, drawing on the experience of soldiers and civilians, from a Lancashire town and a Rhineland village. The book is well illustrated and contains many unique photographs. *£7.95*

ROAD SENSE - Doug Holland

A book for drivers with some experience, preparing them for an advanced driving test. The book introduces a recommended system of car control, based on that developed by the Police Driving School. Doug Holland is a highly qualified driving instructor, working with RoSPA. *£5.95*

TRAINING THE LEARNER DRIVER - Don Gates

The essential guide for all those intending to teach a friend or relation to drive. Written by a drivng professional so that you'll know that you are teaching just the same way as a driving instructor. *£6.95*

WE ALSO PUBLISH:

A new series of investigations into the Supernatural, Myth and Magic:

GHOSTS, TRADITIONS AND LEGENDS OF OLD LANCASHIRE
- Ken Howarth *(£7.95)*

SHADOWS: A northern investigation of the unknown
- Steve Cliffe *(£7.95)*

MYSTERIES OF THE MERSEY VALLEY
- Jenny Randles and Peter Hough *(£7.95)*

Plus, superb illustrated books on Manchester's football teams:

RED FEVER! From Rochdale to Rio as United Supporters *(£7.95)*

MANCHESTER UNITED - Moments to Remember *(£6.95)*

MANCHESTER CITY - Moments to Remember *(£9.95)*

Many more entertaining and educational books are being regularly added to our list. All of our books are available from your local bookshop. In case of difficulty, or to obtain our complete catalogue, please contact:

Sigma Leisure,
1 South Oak Lane, Wilmslow, Cheshire SK9 6AR

Phone: 0625 - 531035 Fax: 0625 - 536800

ACCESS and VISA orders welcome - call our friendly sales staff or use our 24 hour Answerphone service! Most orders are despatched on the day we receive your order - you could be enjoying our books in just a couple of days.